How To
Buy-To-Let Property
Properly:
A guide to property investment

Richard J Oldaker

Bright Pen

A Bright Pen Book

British Library Cataloguing Publication Data.
A catalogue record for this book is available from the British Library

ISBN: 978-0-07552-1567-6

Authors OnLine Ltd
19 The Cinques
Gamlingay, Sandy
Bedfordshire SG19 3NU
England

This book is also available in e-book format, details of which are available at www.authorsonline.co.uk

Disclaimer

This book has been written to give reliable advice to the best of the author's knowledge and experience and cannot be relied upon when making investment decisions. As with any investment, property values can fall as well as rise. The author and publisher disclaim any liability incurred from the use or application of the strategies contained within this book.

The author offers all information as a guide only and it cannot be considered as financial advice in any way. Please refer to your independent financial advisor who is qualified to give you complete advice based on your circumstances. The author is not qualified to give mortgage, legal or financial advice. Please seek legal and financial advice from a qualified advisor before making commitments.

For Emma and Ella. You have given me the strength and happiness to pursue my goals. All you need is a big enough why. You are my why.

About the Author

Richard Oldaker started his career in estate agency in 1997 at the age of 17 and bought his first property 2 years later. He quickly rose to the rank of branch manager and worked for a range of companies up until he started his own Martin & Co lettings franchise with a friend and work colleague in 2009. Their office is based in Aldershot, Hampshire.

He has since built up his own property portfolio whilst gaining the wealth of experience that comes with the letting and day to day management of over 200 client properties.

In his spare time he enjoys socialising with friends, spending time with his wife and daughter, keeping fit, playing guitar and occasionally golf (badly).

Contents

Foreword

I wanted to just very quickly tell you a bit about me and why I feel I have some sort of authority to advise on this subject.

I began my career in estate agency when I was 17 for one of the largest estate agency chains in the UK. I quickly rose to the rank of branch manager and bought my first property at the age of 19. I really wish I had kept that and not sold it after someone told me the market was going to crash, that was in 1999 (they were only 9 years out with their prediction)! I guess that's what happens when you listen to people who don't know what they're talking about!

After 10 years in estate agency (and a bit of buying and selling property) the property crash of 2008 prompted a move into lettings. I am a letting agent day-to-day but continue to expand my property portfolio. I wanted to be in a position whereby my wife didn't have to return to work after giving birth to our beautiful daughter Ella. We achieved a monthly cash flow of £1800 from 4 buy-to-lets which covered all our bills and mortgage on our own house each month. This was achieved before Emma's maternity pay ran out and pretty much replaced her income.

In my early 20's I always felt I was meant for something more, that something special was going to happen to me. I guess the media world can lead you to believe that "something" can just come along and change your life, a lottery win, going in the Big Brother house, X-Factor! I now like to think you make your own luck and things don't change unless you take action.

After marrying Emma in 2008 I sat on the beach whilst on honeymoon and decided I had to change something, I wanted more. I had found the person I wanted to spend the rest of my life with and I wanted us to be happy and financially secure. I knew the best route to this would be working for myself, but I now know that anyone can make money in buy-to-let if they follow some basic rules and principles. I plan to be in a position to be able to retire at 40 (if I choose to), that's in 8 years time. I want to be around whilst Ella (and any other children we may have) grow up. I now read about 2 books a month based around property, business or mind-set and have what my old history teacher always called "a thirst for knowledge". Naturally, we all thought that was bonkers when we were 14! I now understand that what gives me fulfillment is always striving to reach my full potential (and having a wonderful loving family). I used to think I just got bored easily but really I attribute this trait to just wanting to make the most of life and reaching my potential.

If you do what everyone else does, you will get what everyone else gets, and unfortunately, sometimes that isn't a lot. This is why most people will tell you the time to invest in property is over and it can't be done. Only listen to these people if they speak from a position of experience, and even if they have some experience they still might be breaking some of the basic rules summarised at the end of these chapters. I am sure there will be people who will disagree with the views contained in this book. You will always be able to find people who support property investment and those who always seem dead against it (perhaps because of one bad experience when they didn't have the appropriate knowledge). This is only my opinion, but it is based on lots and lots of experience.

We live in a world of 'buy it now', 'get lots of debt', 'don't wait, don't save' and 'worry about it later'. I very nearly fell into the trap of what seems to be the "norm" for society. Buy/rent a house, get married, have children and as your family grows you find yourself needing a bigger property to live in and/or an extra car. You always seem to just get by but don't really have enough money. You may then lose an income when you have kids and if you or your partner needs to go back to work, face massive childcare bills. It can be a vicious cycle which leads to debt for cars, sofas, unexpected bills and holidays you can't afford. I did not, and do not, want this. It all starts with a poor understanding of money and spending beyond your means. If any of this applies to you I urge you to read "The Richest Man in Babylon" by George S Clason, this book shows that good financial principles were used since before Christ was born, and they can still be applied today.

I want to leave a legacy for my children that can look after generations to come and look after Emma and me in our old age. So that's my journey so far. I sincerely hope that you find this book useful.

So who is this book for?

It's for people who want and deserve to reach an element of financial freedom, for people that have worked hard and paid tax all their life and are facing pathetic interest rates on their savings from banks, (the same banks that gambled with their money and then had to be bailed out by the taxpayers). These same banks are demanding higher deposits and implementing stricter criteria for mortgage lending. This book is also for people facing shortfalls in pensions, for young people wondering how they are ever going to get on the property ladder and for people asking themselves, is there another way? It's for people like my parents, my friends and people like you.

This book is aimed at people who want to build a property portfolio of anything from 5 to 10 properties over a reasonable period of time, in a slow, steady and sustained fashion.

There are books out there that talk about building a one million pound property portfolio in a year, or buying as many as one property every 3 or 4 weeks. This approach would fall more under the area of professional full-time investing and, whilst achievable for some, I feel my approach is aimed at the masses who would like to invest but are worried about making the jump. The sort of people who might make some rookie errors if they didn't bother with any research or listened to their mate down the pub who owned one buy-to-let and says it's a nightmare being a landlord.

I have met people with multiple properties who don't know half of what's outlined in this book. I want to stop you making simple errors. Follow my advice and you can achieve a passive income that makes you money while you sleep. Anyone can do it but most people don't, because it is out of their comfort zone. Hopefully you will be more confident and comfortable by the time you finish reading this book.

We change our lives by the decisions we make, some big, some small.

"There are risks and costs to action. But they are far less than the long range risks of comfortable inaction." - John F. Kennedy

1
Why buy-to-let?

I just wanted to go into a bit more depth about why I feel I am qualified to give advice on buy-to-let. I know I mentioned this in the foreword but this is just for those who a) need a bit more convincing or b) didn't read the foreword!

Even the most experienced property investors may have 10, 20, maybe even 50 properties that they let out, either on their own or with the help of a letting agent. Because I own a lettings agency I have the benefit of experience that comes from letting over 150 properties each year. This also means that at one time or another I will have dealt with almost every conceivable problem that comes with owning or managing an investment property. Tenants locking themselves out after office hours, heating not working in winter, bathrooms leaking, roofs leaking, appliances breaking, taps jamming, immersion heaters failing, showers not working, windows leaking, mould problems, gutter problems, fences falling down to name but a few.

This combined with over 10 years as an estate agent before starting a letting agency and owning buy-to-let property means I am well placed to give good advice in a time-efficient way that you can utilise. I don't say any of this for any other reason than to sell you on the idea that I speak from experience. I believe in either sticking to what you know or finding an expert opinion from someone that can be relied on if I am going to invest in an area I don't fully understand. What's more, because I have the estate agency background I can give you some insight as to how they work and some tips on negotiating the best purchase price.

My lettings experience means I can go through the whole process step-by-step, whether you are thinking of using an agent or not. When my business partner James and I started up there was just the two of us. This meant we have both been administrator, property manager, negotiator, and owner. We can do any job role within a lettings agency and as such know how to type an arrears letter to a tenant, negotiate a deal or handle a difficult tenant who doesn't feel its fair for you to hold back some of their deposit on behalf of the landlord.

I hope you find the information contained within these pages useful. Whether you are a first time landlord or more experienced I hope you can take something from this book. It is the same advice that I have given to friends, family and clients who have all made shrewd buy-to-let purchases and made their savings work a bit harder for them and help create an additional income stream from property.

But first things first, is buy-to-let for you?

To buy-to-let (or not buy-to-let)?

Well I'm guessing you think buy-to-let might be for you or you wouldn't have bought this book. However, a lot of people are put off by horror stories and yes there will be the odd one, but with proper procedures in place you can protect yourself from even the worst scenarios imaginable. So, first of all let's have a look at some of the common questions people ask. After all, most people looking to make an investment decision will look at the risk as well as the reward, so what could go wrong...

Will the tenant damage my property?

The honest answer is, well yes they might. But I must stress *might.* Using a decent lettings agent and by referencing tenants properly, you reduce your risk because you are putting tenants in with a good credit history, who are working and, where applicable, you will have a reference from their current/previous landlord. The further you come away from an ideal tenant the more you are increasing your risk. An example would be taking on tenants that rely on local housing allowance (LHA or often known as DSS) as they fall into a higher risk category. Any tenants who couldn't meet credit search criteria or minimum income requirements would also be much higher risk. A deposit will be held in an approved government scheme against any damage, typically a sum equal to 1 1/2 months rent. I will go into much more detail about the whole vetting process later.

What if my tenant doesn't pay?

Again with the strict referencing process you are reducing your risk of non-payment but unforeseen situations occur - people can lose their jobs, relationships end and you do get the occasional professional rent dodger who knows their rights. To give you an idea we have had one court case in four years. That's around 500 moves achieved and 1 eviction, so the chances are low. However, I would still recommend taking a rent guarantee and legal expenses insurance that would cover you in the event of non-payment by a tenant. I have one of these types of policies on all the properties I personally rent out.

What if I can't re-let my property and it sits there empty costing me money?

As of November 2012 void periods in the area I operate are at an all time low, we normally allow around 7 days in between tenancies to allow for any cleaning and decor before the next tenant moves in. The current tenant will have signed a tenancy agreement that requires their co-operation for viewings when it comes to re-letting the property. Even if you get a difficult tenant you, or your lettings agent can insist on entering the property by giving them 24 hours notice, so non-co-operation by a tenant shouldn't be an issue.

Since James and I opened our lettings agency we have been able to re-let every single property. Obviously some are in better condition than others and poor condition is the only thing that would hinder us in re-letting, combined with an inflated asking price. The above is a question I asked myself before extending my portfolio, so I do empathise with Landlords worrying about this. The way I came to terms with this is to ask myself this: If I have managed to keep all of my clients' properties filled with tenants with minimal void periods, then why on earth would it be any different for me? Just one observation on this point though is that it never ceases to amaze how some landlords (although they are few) will leave an empty property sat on the market just to get an extra £25 to £50 a month in rent and have it empty for a month! It's always best to take a £25 or £50 hit and lose £600 maximum over the year rather than lose £800 to £1200 for a whole months rent! But that's just common sense!

What if my rent doesn't cover my mortgage?

The simple answer is, don't buy it. At the moment mortgage lenders will want the rent to cover the mortgage by 125% so they won't let you buy if the rent doesn't cover the mortgage. The purpose of getting into this buy-to-let malarkey is to make a bit of profit and get a better return than you would in the bank, as well as buying in at a competitive price to ensure some capital growth.

What if my tenant is constantly phoning me with problems?

If you have a managing agent then they won't be calling you at all. We will look at this in more depth later in terms of what service levels you should expect and receive from your agent. If you are managing the tenancy yourself you can minimise phone calls by being very thorough and providing a "Move-in Pack" explaining how things work. You should include appliance manuals, information on where the stop cock is, the boiler manual, how to tackle condensation and information on ventilation, where the fuse box is etcetera. Leaving a welcome bottle of wine doesn't do any harm either! You will also need to know a good local plumber, electrician and maintenance company "Handyman", unless you are handy and can do the maintenance yourself (and have the time)! Do not tackle anything to do with gas or electrics unless you have the necessary qualifications.

Why should you buy-to-let?

Now let's have a look at why you should put your money into buy-to-let.

At the time of writing interest rates have been low for over 4 years meaning savers have been hit hard. For people with substantial sums in savings, for example £50,000, a 2.5% return earns them just over £100 per month. If you have similar savings, consider this: What if I could show you a way of getting at least 5% net yield on property and capital growth and a return on investment of 8% plus per year? Well with interest rates on mortgages the way they are at the moment, it isn't that difficult. To save you some time I have done some due diligence for you, although you will naturally have to do your own research extensively I will back up what I am saying with a couple of real examples detailed a bit later in this chapter.

My own motivation for buy-to-let investment is to build a residual income off the back of investment property. If I can turn each £35,000 to £50,000 I can save, or release, from property by way of remortgage into a monthly income of £300 to £500 *and* have the benefit of capital growth *and* negotiate hard and buy in a 10% discount off market value then I will be set for retirement. Also, all the time I'm working, I have two income streams. This is particularly good as a back up for anyone who is employed. In these turbulent times unemployment and redundancies are high. I think that the biggest reason why people don't get involved in this is that their lack of knowledge creates fear. Both I, friends and family members would have been buying property to let out long ago if we knew then what we know now. I have been able to help make the process easy through my recent experience as a Lettings Agent and therefore reduced the fear of getting involved in something that they perhaps feel they should know more about. I hope this book can act in that same capacity for you.

Think about this, if you are reading this and you are in the age category of 40-50+, what would your life be like now if you had bought 5 properties before you were 35? Regardless of what the market has done, you would have done well wouldn't you? What did properties cost when you were in your 20's? How much would they be worth now? How different would your life and retirement be? Well, it isn't too late. **It is never too late.** You can start now and who knows, you might live to a 100. You can pass on the wealth you create to future generations and still create a comfortable retirement.

If you are reading this and you are under 40 you have plenty of time to make a difference for yourself, your children and your retirement. Start now - well, once you have finished reading!

Let inflation reduce your debt

Now I'm not saying debt is "good" but money devalues over time - fact. A pint of milk in 1980 was around 17p and the average house price was just shy of £23,000. So if I can build a £1million property portfolio with a debt of £750,000 I can wait for the house prices to double regardless of whether that is 10,15 or 20 years. I can then sell £1million worth of property and clear all the debt and have a nice income. I will end up with £1million worth of property unencumbered that cost me £250,000 in deposits. If you can buy under market value then you will have been able to get a lot of that £250,000 back out of the properties on re-mortgage. The result? A £1 million property portfolio for nothing! All it takes is time, knowledge and some money for the deposits. Or if you're young enough you can wait 30-40 years and £750,000 won't be difficult to pay off at all and you can keep all the properties which will probably be worth £4-5 million plus.

Leverage

Buying with mortgages is leveraging other people's money (the bank or building society's money). They are happy, if you fit their criteria, to lend you the majority of the cash needed to buy a property and in return just require their interest payment. They do not demand a share of the profit or a share of the rent, just the payment on the interest. Can you think of any other type of investment where someone will put in most of the money and require no equity stake or profit share? I can't.

The property cycle

Understanding the basic property cycle is key to understanding when it's the right time to buy and when might be the right time to sell. Whilst buy-to-let should only be considered as a long term form of investment it can be good to have some kind of exit plan – we'll talk a little about this later.

The property cycle can be broken down into the four stages that are outlined starting on the next page. The cycle typically takes 18 years to run before it repeats itself. This 18 year boom bust cycle is well documented and has been highly researched; let's quickly look back at the last 100 or so years. You will see that each of these points in history are 18 years apart.

2008: Financial crises, recession that we recently experienced that people may argue we are now out of.

1990: Property prices crash following boom of late 1980's – prices hit rock bottom in 1992.

1972: Oil crisis, worst global economic output since the great depression (of 1936).

1954: House prices dropped, national debt was enormous following WWII

1936: In the midst of the great depression.

At these 18 year landmarks above we saw house prices "bottom out" and the cycle start over.

The following section gives a little more detail on the different stages of the 18 year cycle, including some signs to watch out for to help you correctly identify whether the cycle has naturally moved onto its next phase.

Stage One – The Stealth Phase
This is the first stage following a crash and can typically last for four to five years. House price increases will be virtually non-existent. Confidence amongst buyers is very low, as it is with lenders, banks and other financial institutions. People are worried about any further price drops or the threat of a "double dip", sound familiar? We officially had a double dip recession in 2012.

Stage Two – Awareness Phase
By this point some time has passed since the initial crash. Smart investors will have realised that the housing market has in fact reached rock bottom and will start to buy investment property. The rate at which investors buy is down to their own financial circumstances and their attitude to risk. I believe we are now in this phase. This "awareness" phase will again typically last a further four to five years. This is the stage that you want to be involved and ideally no later than this stage. You still need to be looking at getting good discounts off asking prices and let the returns dictate what you consider to be a good investment.

Stage Three – Mania Phase

The initial bust period is now a distant memory. Consumer confidence has returned. Banks have had time to recover. Smart investors have been buying up property successfully. First time buyers are back on the scene competing with investors. The media start to report increasing house prices and jump on the bandwagon of an increasing housing market. I remember in the last boom the media reporting that house prices were going up more per day than what most people could earn in a day. First time landlords start buying. There is a sense of urgency to buy and not get left behind before prices increase further.

Stage Four – Crash/Blowout Phase

House prices have increased too much as a result of the "Mania" stage. People have over-borrowed and banks have lent beyond their means. House prices have increased at a rate that has far outpaced inflation and wage increases. Then comes the crash.

So what is the conclusion here? Well it is my feeling that we have just entered the awareness phase so now is a great time to get involved.

An overview of my views on property investing in the buy-to-let market

The last buy-to-let boom went really crazy from about 2005 up until the crash in 2008. This is where people were entirely reliant on increasing prices so they could pull out the equity to buy the next one and weren't concerned with a residual monthly income. It was all reliant on the housing market continuing to go up. At that time Northern rock were offering 125% mortgages and having a 5% deposit was considered a good thing, having a deposit at all from a first time buyer was rare. In fact first time buyers were being encouraged to take 125% of the property's value, consolidate all their debt and buy. And we wonder why it all went wrong! Buy-to-let deposits were around 15% at the time and in some cases 10%. That, combined with the high property prices meant you couldn't make a monthly profit (cash flow) when putting very little money into the deal. Often, people who made poor investment purchases had to top up the rent with their own money to meet the mortgage payments. Not a good or sustainable strategy.

The main parts of my own strategy are as follows:

- Always make sure I have 25% equity in my buy-to-lets, even if the minimum requirement drops. That way I am protected against any further (although unlikely at the moment) drop in property prices.
- Is to only ever release equity when I can take out a decent amount (enough for another deposit on another investment property or enough to go in on a joint venture) *and* leave 25% equity in.
- The investment must result in a minimum 7% Gross Yield (more about yields later) or I won't buy it. Don't get emotional or buy as if you were going to live in the property, do the numbers and look at the return.

Here is an example of a property I bought in October 2011. It is a 2 bedroom ex-council house in Hampshire and it caught my eye because my company had let a similar property two doors down for another landlord. It had been on the market for some time at £150k. I offered £130k, which was rejected. I went up to 135k which was also rejected. I walked away, the agent contacted me again a couple of weeks later as the price had dropped to £145k, I resubmitted £135k for a quick purchase and it was accepted.

The sums look like this:

Purchase price £135,000
Deposit £33,750
Decor, some cheap carpets and some appliances £2,596.93
Stamp duty and solicitors costs £2,150

Total expenditure £38,496.93

The property was rented before my first mortgage payment at £825 per month (the surveyor said it was worth £775 on his valuation, they do tend to err on the side of caution).

£825 x 12(months) = £9,900 divided by purchase price of £135,000 = **7.33% Gross Yield**

My buy-to-let mortgage had a £1,995 arrangement fee added to the loan making my mortgage amount £103,245. The interest rate was 3.89% making my mortgage payment £334.69 a month or £4,016.23 per year. My buildings insurance is £30 per month putting my costs up to £4,376.23. This gives me £460 a month profit.

My return on investment therefore is:
Rent £9,900 - £4,376.23 Yearly costs = £5523.77 Profit.
£5523.77 Profit divided by £38,497 (total property expenditure) = 0.14348.
You then multiply this figure by 100 to get a percentage
= **14.35% Return on investment (ROI).**

I don't charge myself a management fee but let's factor in a monthly fee of 10% to take into account Letting Agent's fees.

Costs
10% managed fee for letting agent plus VAT = £99
Other initial start up costs such as inventory, gas safety certificate means we would add £500 to your initial costs.
So my total expenditure of £38,497 would become £38,997 if I paid an agent.

Yearly outgoing with agency fee becomes £5,564.23. This would give a monthly income of £361.31

Your ROI would be more like 11.12%. A bit better than the 2.5% I was getting in my ING savings!

Many people are happy to offer advice about property but often it won't even include the most important thing - the return. It's different if you are buying a house to live in, your dream house or your 'forever' house but when buying-to-let you must not forget the purchase is an investment, so the numbers need to come first. Here is a simple chart that can at least take care of the yield side of things.

This following chart should represent a worst case scenario in terms of cash flow as I have based the rent on only a 6% yield and factored in only a 25% deposit and a buy-to-let mortgage deal of 4.5%. At the time of writing there are considerably better deals out there than 4.5%. I have also factored in 1% stamp duty, a 10% managed or rent collect service fee plus VAT at the prevailing rate. You need to look at what is an achievable rental price versus the purchase price and the challenge is to see if you can improve on these numbers (which should be possible).

Purchase Price	Monthly Rent	Mortgage amount	Monthly Mortgage	Profit after agents cost
£250,000	£1250	£187,500	£703.13	£396.87
£225,000	£1125	£168,750	£632.70	£357.30
£200,000	£1000	£150,000	£562.50	£317.50
£175,000	£875	£131,250	£492.19	£277.81
£150,000	£750	£112,500	£421.88	£238.12
£125,000	£625	£93,750	£351.56	£198.44
£100,000	£500	£75,000	£281.25	£158.75

The challenge is to see if you can improve on the figures above, use this chart as minimum specification for your investments. To back up what can be achieved here is another example, a property bought in Surrey, one of the most expensive areas in the country.

This was a property I negotiated on behalf of a family member. I was very stubborn with not increasing on the offer, even when the agent asked for just another £500. I started at £95,000 and ended up agreeing at £100,000 for a 1 bedroom Charles Church built flat. This property had a tenant in-situ so I organised liaising with them and keeping them in the loop as well as making sure the rent came to us instead of the old agent once the transaction had gone through. The original rent was £570, perhaps a little under market value at the time and this has been increased to £600 per month on renewal.

So the figures on this example are:

£100,000 Purchase price
£40,000 Deposit
£60,000 Mortgage at 3.95% interest rate = £2,370 per annum mortgage
£197.50 per month
Purchasing costs including solicitors and survey fee were £850
Total cost of purchase £40,850
Management Company costs for maintaining gardens and communal areas is £480 per year, this includes building insurance.
Monthly fees to letting agent are £54.72 including VAT so £656.64 per year.

Rent income £6,840
Outgoings £3,506.64
Profit before tax £3,333.36
Monthly Profit £277.78.

Gross yield is 6.84% (Rental income as a percentage of the purchase price).

ROI is 8.16%. To clarify ROI is the amount of money you make represented as a percentage of the total money you had to outlay to buy the property.

The ROI is a bit lower here because more cash was invested meaning a lower loan to value. This will normally mean a better mortgage rate but because you are tying up more cash in the property your ROI goes down. Sometimes less is more, make your money work harder for you by only putting in a 25% deposit, you can then make more purchases.

It is also worth mentioning that this flat was bought by the previous owner for £139,000 in September 2007 so we should see some decent capital growth even if it doesn't go back to those heights!

Are the desired yields and returns possible in your area?

Here is an exercise I think you should do for yourself, right now. I have carried it out in 3 random areas in the country to see if this method can be applied anywhere. I am going to use a 2 bedroom house for my example as they tend to let well and there are no management company charges to factor in (because they are Freehold) like you would have to consider with a flat. Lets see if property prices and rents stack up. Remember, let the numbers dictate your decision to buy. Use the notes section at the back to get on the internet now and test your preferred areas.

I am going to pick Basildon, as I was born there, Peterborough because my brother lives there and Swansea because my sister went to university there. So once you have picked your area/s go to a website like rightmove.co.uk and check the rent versus house price. We can probably assume that given the current market the properties aren't going for asking price. I think it is fair to assume you will be able to get at least a 5% discount off asking prices but I will base my figures on asking prices anyway. I will also use the asking prices quoted on "Let

Agreed" properties. I hope you will notice that I am being consistently over-cautious on the numbers in the hope to convince you buy-to-let is a sound investment strategy.

So here we go...

Example 1: Basildon

I have put into rightmove.co.uk "2 bed, house" only. Using our guide I am going to see if you can buy anything for less than £160,000 and get a rent of £800 plus.

This has returned 183 result so I am going to view from "lowest price first".

There seems to be a few 2 and 3 bedroom houses coming in at about £110,000 to £115,000. This is looking promising although it seems clear these aren't the most sought after areas. Remember, anything will let at the right price as long as the condition is good enough, in the same way that anything will sell at the right price!

Here is a good example, the property has been repossessed because the selling agent has published the current offer price (more on buying repossessions later).

Notice Of Offer Chatfield Way, Basildon, Essex, SS13 2BN
We advise that an offer has been made for the above property in the sum of £114,000.
Key features:

Three Bedrooms
Terraced
Gas Central Heating
Close To Amenities

The good thing about this is I have the full postcode so can narrow down my search for comparable rental properties by searching by postcode and a ¼ or ½ mile radius. You must make sure that the rental properties you use for pricing are on the same estate or in a very similar location. I don't want to over estimate this by using properties in a more desirable area and therefore producing an unrealistic projection. But remember, I believe in sticking to what you know, so know your area and research it well. I am doing this exercise to prove the formula can work anywhere in the country.

So having searched "SS13 2BN" Houses minimum of 2 bedrooms, 3 bedrooms maximum within a ¼ mile I have 5 results. The cheapest being a 2 bedroom house at £725 and the most expensive being a 3 bedroom house at £900 with 1 of the 5 houses being "Let Agreed" at £750 PCM.

So lets be really conservative in our analysis here. Lets say I get a 2 bedroom house for £115,000, which seems very achievable, and I let it for £650, there are many 2 bedroom houses "Let Agreed" at this figure if I increase my "SS13 2BN" search to a ½ mile radius. How does this look compared to the chart detailed earlier? As you can see, £115,000 purchase price and a rent of £650 compares very favourably.

£115,000 purchase price
£86,250 mortgage amount
£323.44 a month mortgage
£78 agent's fees inc vat per month
£248.56 profit a month

Gross Yield 6.78%
Cost of purchase (remember no stamp duty at this figure)!
Deposit £28,750
Solicitors & Survey £1,000

Inventory and set-up fee for agent, gas certificate, electrical check £500
£2,000 on incidentals (decoration or kitchen appliances for example).
Total cost of purchase £32,250

Yearly profit divided by total cost of purchase = 9.25% return on your money annually!

I will shorten the example of my other 2 areas and just tell you how the figures work out.

Example 2, Peterborough

2 Bedroom House
Purchase price £80,000 seems very achievable, in fact a lot that are sold at asking prices of £75,000.
Rent - A real range here from £500 to £600 so lets base it on £500.
Gross Yield is 7.5%
Cost of purchase is £23,000
Profit for year is £2,580
ROI is 11.22%

I would be very aware that the potential for capital growth is exponentially higher in London and the South East and South West. There may be other city centers and areas earmarked for redevelopment that may also prove to be a wise place to invest so I appreciate saying "London and the South is best for Capital growth" is somewhat of a blanket statement but you won't go wrong if you know your area and do your research. Some people who have bought properties in places like Peterborough have seen no price increases whatsoever over the last 8 years and you really do want to be aiming to achieve capital growth. However, you may decide that the better yield and return on investment still make it attractive. Avoiding stamp duty and having to find less cash to put down as a deposit could mean you can build a portfolio quicker, diversify with 1, 2 and 3 bedroom properties in different city locations and thus spread your risk.

Example 3, Swansea

I have chosen the postcode SA1 for my search.
2 Bedroom House
Purchase price £80,000.
Rent - A real range here from £375 to £525 but with only 1 in 25 properties marked as "Let Agreed" alarm bells ring so lets base it on £375!
Gross Yield is 5.63%
Cost of purchase is £23,000
Profit for year is £1,260
ROI is 5.47%

These numbers don't look so good. What you would have to do is make a purchase at around £65,000 which could be achievable if you have patience. That is the only way the returns would be worth it in this area. I'm sure a yearly profit of £1,260 doesn't do much to whet your appetite! This is why you must let the numbers dictate. I would never consider a gross yield of less than 6% but if I had to pay agents' fees then I would be after 6.5% minimum.

Still not convinced?

Let's have a quick look at property versus shares. You can do your own research on how the share market has performed over time and I think its around a 5% increase per year on average. Like property it has had its market crashes.

Property has dropped by around 20% since the height in 2007 with the majority of this happening over the course of about a year. So if you have 25% in each property then you are protected and, in time, you will still win in property.

However I'm sure you have seen or heard the news when a big company has 20% wiped of its value IN A DAY! That is just staggering. I think I can just about get my head around a property (or portfolio) going down by 20% over the course of a year, at least you have some time to adjust and plan your next move, get cash flow in place, increase rent etcetera. But to lose 20% in a day must be just gut-wrenching. Do you remember the BP oil spill in 2010? The share price nearly halved! Tescos shares dropped by about 20% (in a day) earlier in 2012 after some poor results were announced. Facebook shares at the time of writing are <u>half</u> what they were at flotation only a few months ago! I'm sorry but that is just far too volatile for me. I would be a nervous wreck. Plus I don't have the time to spend becoming an expert in that field!

People say you can't get out of property quickly if you need to, which is true. But you can release money relatively quickly if needed and borrow against property. As with any investment that goes down, you only lose money if you sell.

Look at the following chart for a plan to buy 5 properties, over 5 years. The price increases are based on 5% growth on the property purchase price per year, well under all historical trends.

	Year 1	Year 2	Year 3	Year 4	Year 5
Property 1	£100,000	£105,000	£110,250	£115,763	£121,551
Property 2		£100,000	£105,000	£110,250	£115,763
Property 3			£100,000	£105,000	£110,250
Property 4				£100,000	£105,000
Property 5					£100,000

If you do nothing else but this, you will have made £52,564 in equity. Leave all 5 properties for another 5 years and the chart looks like this (again at only 5% growth).

	Year 6	Year 7	Year 8	Year 9	Year 10
Property 1	£127,628	£134,009	£140,709	£147,744	£155,131
Property 2	£121,551	£127,628	£134,009	£140,709	£147,744
Property 2	£115,763	£121,551	£127,628	£134,009	£140,709
Property 4	£110,250	£115,763	£121,551	£127,628	£134,009
Property 5	£105,000	£110,250	£115,763	£121,551	£127,628

This now makes your total capital growth £206,221. The great thing about this is if you follow my rules and strategy outlined later then you will be able to release equity from property number 1 to buy property number 3 and then property number 2 to buy property number 4 and then property number 3 to buy property number 5. This is based on the fact that you are most likely going to be looking at a 2 year mortgage deal. Also if you can buy in at a £10,000 discount and then add £10,000 value, then factor in 2 years capital growth you should be able to re-mortgage and pull out enough money to put 25% down on another £100,000 property and pay for your fees. All whilst leaving 25% in your property. For example:

Purchase price £100,000
Real Value £110,000
Market Value after minimal refurbishment £120,000
Capital growth after 2 years at 5%per annum £132,300
Re-mortgage to 75% Loan to Value (LTV) leaves a mortgage of £99,225 releasing £33,075 for your next purchase.

I plan to do the above whilst saving as well to increase the rate of purchase. I have income from my business/job, rental income and can release equity to fund property purchases. I am really just starting out on my property investment journey but already I can see why people who have money find it easier to accumulate more – they buy income generating assets. It is easy to see why "The rich get richer and the poor get poorer". Money creates money.

Summary

- Research your local area
- Base decisions on numbers, not emotions
- If the numbers don't stack, don't buy it
- Understand the property cycle
- Let inflation reduce your debt

Observe the masses and do the opposite, remember what happened to all those people who jumped on the band wagon buying off-plan from 2005 to 2007? They lost money, got into negative equity and some got repossessed.

2
Finding the right property

So you have decided to go ahead and venture into the world of property investment and buy-to-let. One of the main ingredients needed now is money for a deposit.

Depending on your purchase price you might only need £20,000 for a 25% deposit or you might need £50,000. Regardless of what you need there are various ways of going about it. Here are the main ones.

Equity Release

This is going to be the easiest route for people with equity in their property. It can still seem scary, especially for those who have been working to pay off their mortgage. Just don't forget to let inflation reduce your debt! This is straightforward, if you have 40% or 30% equity in your home you re-mortgage to a higher amount, provided you can borrow more. For example, you have a £200,000 property with a £120,000 mortgage. You re-mortgage up to 75% LTV leaving you with a £150,000 mortgage and £30,000 in the bank for your investment property, simple.

Saving

Many of you reading this may be familiar with the concept of "paying yourself first". This may sound a little weird. After all you have bills, mortgage, council tax, food and petrol to shell out for. What this means is that you should take 10% of what you earn and save it. You take the 10% before any bills are paid, even credit card or loan debt. You must adjust your spending to the 10/20/70 ratio. That is 10% save, 20% on past debt (loans, credit cards) and 70% to be spent on your day-to-day living and other bills. Big purchases and gratification must wait. Pay your most costly debts off first, (normally credit cards) followed by the debts with lower interest rates. This does not include mortgage debt as your mortgage debt will be covered by your rent.

This is massively powerful and even for people who have debt it can have a huge positive effect on your mindset. Even though you're still in debt you might be saving £200 per month. So in 6 months you have £1,200 in savings whereas before you had nothing and spent all you earned. You will find ways to cut back if you try and as your debt eases you might increase to saving 20% or even 30%. Try it, it could change your life. This is one of the principles outlined in "The Richest Man in Babylon".

Room Renting

In the first house I ever lived in that I owned I rented out two rooms to friends. This nearly covered my mortgage enabling me to save consistently and have a good lifestyle. This is another option and I would strongly recommend it to anyone who is serious about buying a second property as an investment and making sure their future and retirement is not just like everyone else's. This approach, combined with a small equity release, enabled me to keep this property and buy another with my wife.

Borrowing

This is another good option. You could perhaps do a joint venture with a friend or relative where they provide you with an interest-free loan which you can repay out of your share of the rental profit. This could be in return for you doing all the research and finding a good property at a good price, liaising with the estate agents and negotiating the deal. If your potential partner is in doubt, suggest they read this book and discuss the pros and cons after.

Now to get searching

Now that you know the numbers, have the deposit and have decided to go ahead, you need to find a property. Now they say its all about location, location, location. But I say its about the deal. You can tell already that if the numbers don't stack then I don't buy. Some may criticise that approach because this may not take into account up and coming locations, areas of redevelopment, or parts of inner cities that are considered a bad bet, or an area from which investors tend to steer clear.

If you have done your research on the local area, spoken to estate and lettings agents then you will know whether buying in a certain location is bad. As you saw in my earlier example I have a 2 bedroom ex-council house in my portfolio and although it wouldn't be my first choice of a place to live, the figures stacked up very well and I am convinced I managed to buy in at least a £10,000 discount. My business partner has also bought a 2 bedroom ex-council house this year because the numbers stack (8.3% yield) and the size is good.

The type of property that can make a really good deal is one that is in cosmetically poor condition e.g. old carpets and decoration. If this is combined with a reasonable kitchen and bathroom and a modern boiler (or a boiler that has been regularly serviced) then this could be a good property to negotiate on. People who are not buying for investment find it harder to see through this kind of condition. If the property is dirty and messy, then all the better. You and I know that new carpets and a full schedule of redecoration throughout can cost as little as a few thousand pounds but the property will be vastly improved once this work has been carried out. These are the sorts of places where you can get £10,000-£15,000 (or more) off the asking price just because the owner is too lazy, or can't afford to pay attention to presentation. Poor cleanliness and the property being untidy is also good for you as it will put off other buyers.

Other areas to look for include a modern fuse box and up-to-date wiring; the condition of any flat roofs or old slate roofs if buying an older property; noise from neighbours through walls or ceiling if a flat. Look at the condition of the neighbours and surrounding properties, do they give off a good impression? Think about road noise from main roads or motorways, the location of any nearby water works can leave an unpleasant aroma in the air. Also is there anything unsightly with the outlook or within close proximity to the property? These factors combined with "the deal" make more difference than if it's close to a bus or railway station (in my opinion). You don't want to end up with someone else's nightmare property that can't be resold!

There are exceptions to most rules so if your research has shown you get a considerably higher yield if the property is on a certain development or walking distance to a mainline train station then do look for a property that meets this criteria but not at the expense of the other items listed above.

In the area where I work and live properties without any parking can be very difficult to let. This may not be the case in London where fewer people have cars and rely solely on the tube and bus services. But anywhere else, watch out. Buying a property on a main road where you have to park a 2 minute walk away is not going to help let the property and in my experience parking is a priority for tenants. It can also be worse if the surrounding roads are permit holders only. You might find you have to significantly reduce your asking price or look at a housing benefit tenant to get the place let.

Freehold and Leasehold

I think it is important to explain the difference between Freehold and Leasehold as this could have a major influence on whether you buy a particular property. You will often see either "Freehold" or "Leasehold" after the price on the front of estate agents property particulars but people don't always know what they mean. If you do, skip this bit. Read on if you think you might not know all there is to know.

Essentially, houses are freehold, you are buying the freehold of the property and the land that it sits on. You will realise the advantage of this when you read on about the pitfalls of short leases. Don't get me wrong, there is nothing wrong with leasehold and the first property I ever bought was leasehold but there are things to watch out for.

A flat is leasehold because you can't own the ground that it sits on because the properties are stacked on top of one another. So what you are buying is the lease for your part of that building. There is still a Freeholder or "landlord" as it will state in the lease and you are buying a lease to occupy the property for the number of years remaining on the lease. The lease is a legal document that outlines a number of complex legal matters but the most important content is the length of the lease. Common lengths of lease start at 99 years, 125 Years and 999 Years and decrease over time. The reason this is so important is because mortgage lenders require a specific number of years to be remaining on the lease once the mortgage term has expired, normally 30 to 35 years. Some lenders have a cut-off and won't lend on a property with less than 70 years remaining at the time of purchase. For example if you are taking a mortgage term of 30 years and the lender requires 30 years remaining on the lease when you buy it then the lease must have a minimum of 60 years remaining when you buy the property. With a mortgage of 35 years, it may need to be a 70 year lease when you purchase! This means that if the lease had an original length of 99 years the property could only be 30 years old and be difficult to mortgage. This poses another issue of having to think about how long you are going to own the property for, even before you've bought it, because if the lease drops too low then resale could be a problem.

Freeholders

Blocks of leasehold flats will have a freeholder. This can be an individual or a management company acting on behalf of the freeholder who might be a company. If it is an individual a management company is often employed to maintain the building, organise window cleaning and look after communal gardens. There will be a service charge payable of anything from a negligible amount of ground rent to over £300 a month (although this upper end is more likely in London). The properties that have no maintenance charge and just a ground rent tend to have the freehold owned by a council or housing association. A friend of mine has a one bedroom modern flat in Hampshire and pays £70 per month and I would say that this is fairly typical unless you are looking at expensive gated developments or exclusive areas. The estate agent will be able to clarify lease length and maintenance charges to you when you enquire about the flat. Maintenance charges paid to the management company or freeholder cannot be charged to the tenant so it is important you know what they are and take the total cost from your annual rent when calculating your yield. Don't forget that the market dictates rental prices so you can't just put the rent up by £50 to £100 to cover the additional maintenance charges. Personally I would only buy leasehold if my ground rent and maintenance charges were under £50 per month. This cost will include the insurance for your building so you do save some money there but high maintenance charges can really injure your profit margins. Stick to a minimum 6% yield after these charges and you won't go far wrong.

You must be wary about consistently increasing maintenance charges. They will tend to creep up over time and there is not much you can do about it without going down a lengthy legal route called the Leasehold Valuation Tribunal (LVT) that makes decisions on various types of dispute relating to residential leasehold property.

Local Councils as Freeholders

A quick note about local councils as freeholders. Councils don't tend to charge much maintenance, and ground rent may be negligible but they have been known to schedule works on block of flats and then present the leaseholders with an estimated bill of thousands, and I mean THOUSANDS! If this does occur then the leaseholders can go down the LVT route but it could still mean an unexpected bill of a few thousand. That might not be a major issue if you are getting something in return like double glazed windows but some councils have been known (at the time of writing) to have profit share deals in place with preferred contractors. So, you, the leaseholder pay your bill in full and the council gets a sort of "cash back" from the contractor, sounds criminal doesn't it?!

Ground rent

This is quite literally a fee for renting the ground. It is normally a nominal amount and I would say £50-£250 for the year would be typical in my experience. This doesn't tend to vary as hugely as maintenance charges do but could be more than this in London.

Absentee Freeholders

Absentee freeholders are not uncommon but can cause massive complications when it comes to renewing a lease. If a freeholder can't be located then they can't be approached to enter into negotiations if a lease needs renewing. There is also the added danger of them reappearing and wanting to claim back years of unpaid ground rent. If you are considering buying a flat and your solicitor discovers there is an absentee freeholder I would proceed with caution. It is a lengthy legal process (approx 6 months) to get a lease extended with an absentee freeholder and it means instructing a specialist solicitor who has to go to court and also prove they have tried to track down the freeholder. Make sure any properties are bought at a significant discount. I suggest 25%-30% below market value. Don't forget that even if, after taking advice, you are happy that an absentee freeholder isn't a problem to you personally, that doesn't necessarily mean the next person you sell to will think the same. Remember, it doesn't matter how much a property is valued at, its only worth what someone is prepared to pay and that could be limited if there is something legal hanging over the property that could jeopardise a sale.

Renewing a lease

When it comes to renewing a lease it is the freeholder who is paid for the renewal. Now this is an extremely specialised area when it comes to negotiating a new lease and the calculation used to establish price. All I can tell you is that from my experience it is not cheap. To give you an idea, most lease renewal prices that I have heard are around the £10,000-£15,000 mark. I know this because I have spoken to people whilst conducting valuations in my estate agent days who were stuck in a position where they can neither sell (because of the low lease) nor afford to pay for a renewal. Often the only way out is to sell at a knocked-down price to a cash buyer. I once heard of a rogue freeholder who was being obstructive with the renewing of leases so he could try and buy all the flats back way under market value. The lower a lease is, the more expensive it is to renew.

My Solicitors advise to investigate what a renewal would cost if a lease is 80 years or less. So, in some cases a flat might only be 19 years old and the Solicitor is potentially warning you off it! This may seem crazy but if you want my advice I would be making sure I had a strategy in place to either sell the property early when the lease was still okay, renew the lease straight away or wait it out for 15-20 years and renew the lease then. By which time the property will have significantly grown in value.

999 year leases

Properties with this length of lease are a much safer bet. The first flat I owned had a balance of a 999 year lease, so no renewal cost or trouble with selling for me! The scenario of a 999 year lease normally occurs when each individual owner of the flats have got together to buy out the freeholder. This can normally be a nice sum of money for the freeholder but can typically be about the £3,000-£4,000 mark for each owner. The owners will then pay a solicitor to renew the lease to 999 years at cost price and create their own management company or all agree on one to instruct. This means they then have control over the day-to-day running of the block and have enhanced future saleability with the lengthy lease. Alternatively they may not decide to renew the lease immediately as they are only ever going to charge themselves the cost of the legal work and not have to pay a renewal fee that a normal freeholder would ordinarily want.

More and more builders are following the trend of giving new apartment blocks 125 year leases (as they own the freehold they can decide the length of the lease). This enhances saleability and gives the option of buying for a long-term investment enabling you to sell on even 30-40 years down the line with no trouble due to lease length.

Communal areas

If you do end up looking at buying a leasehold flat then have a look at the communal hallways and other communal areas. This will give you an idea what the freeholder or managing agent is doing with the monthly maintenance fees (if anything). Communal hallways should be clean, security entry phone systems should be working and the building secure. Are the carpets and walls damaged or marked? If so when are they next scheduled to be decorated? When was this last done? Feel free to ask questions of anyone you see coming and going, are they owners or tenants? If owners, how have they found the management company? Are the gardens regularly tended to in the growing season? Are the windows clean? You get the picture, ask questions, do research, be diligent.

Do I buy old or new?

I'm going to start sounding like a broken record because, it depends on the deal. At the time of writing my oldest property is the 1960's ex-council house. The first flat I bought was a Victorian conversion which I have since sold. There are definitely more things to look out for when buying older. However some of these tips will apply on anything over 20 years old.

Damp

This is quite common in older properties as there is no cavity wall. This should not be confused with mould that can occur due to condensation because of a lack of ventilation or adequate heating. Rising damp will occur where the damp course has failed and/or the ground level outside is higher than the damp course or the air bricks are either 1) not present or 2) blocked. You can smell damp and you can often see it. Look out for bubbling paint around bay windows. Look at the ground level outside and ask if any damp works have been done and if so, are they under guarantee. Also is that guarantee transferable with the ownership of the property. You can get a damp, dry rot, wood worm specialist report normally free of charge from a local company. Have a look at a website like checkatrade.com or ratedpeople.com to find a recommended local company.

Have a look at the roof, is it an original slate roof? Are there tiles missing? Have a look at the pointing and also the state of the chimney stack. I would always recommend a more in depth survey on an older property and would select a "Homebuyers" survey which is much more in depth than the basic mortgage valuation. If it is a property that you are taking on with a view to doing work or want to be extra safe then get a full structural survey done. Prices will vary depending on purchase price and size of property.

Surveyors won't test services or inspect gas or electrics. You can get a plumber and electrician to look over these things for you before committing to an offer or if you have already had an offer accepted, get them checked before exchange of contracts. The main areas to consider when buying old is structure, damp and roof. Gut feel and a decent survey should steer you from trouble and I think with a close look most people will get a feel for whether someone has done a quick patch up job to do up and sell on or if some real TLC has gone into a place.

Don't forget there are various websites available where you can see how much someone has paid for a property and when they bought it, try:

www.rightmove.co.uk
www.zoopla.co.uk

So I guess the real answer is it doesn't matter whether you buy old or new but there is definitely more to watch out for with older. Just make sure you don't get caught out with a large bill for any of the above mentioned potential problems.

Repossessions

Occasionally when you are looking for a property you may encounter one that has been repossessed by the mortgage company. This has become increasingly more common in recent times as you can see from the Basildon example I used earlier. Sometimes the estate agent will let you know that it is a repossessed property because different procedures apply. These procedures may vary slightly depending on who is dealing with it and I will explain these later.

In most cases the lender will appoint an asset management company to deal with the estate agent. They will take a fee and then the estate agent will get a fee. The fee the estate agent gets for dealing with a repossession is normally quite low 1% +vat is typical, if they are lucky they might get 1.25%+vat. There are certain rules that have to be adhered to, and knowing these may help you if you looking to buy a repossessed property.

In my experience all repossessed properties have to be advertised in the paper at least twice before any offer other than the asking price (or over) can be accepted. If your offer is accepted you will have to exchange contracts within 28 days if buying with a mortgage, or 14 days if you are a cash buyer. There is often a few days leeway with this because it wouldn't be in the lenders best interest to pull the plug on a sale if you were nearly ready to exchange but the deadline had expired, so don't panic too much!

Repossessed properties tend to be marketed at more attractive prices and the reasons for this in my experience would be as follows;

People having their homes repossessed are going to be in arrears with their mortgage payments, often have high debt and so looking after their home is not always priority. It has also been known for people to trash the house before leaving.

When an estate agent is filling out the mortgage lenders paperwork following receipt of the keys on a repossessed property mortgage lenders ask for a 2-4 week sale price, a 6-8 week sale price and a 12 week sale price. The 2-4 week is considered a forced sale price, they want to know what the bottom line is. My personal opinion on this was that, as estate agents, we had to do so much more paperwork and got such a low commission that I was only too happy to put a figure on a property that meant at least it sold quickly! At the end of the day, repossession is last resort and mortgage lenders want their money back.

This is an area that can be open to corruption by estate agents and although mortgage lenders are putting more and more procedures in place to clamp down on this, it does still happen. Typical warning signs to look out for are if the estate agent says the property has already gone. Repossessions must be marketed up until exchange of contracts and displaying a for sale board outside is always insisted upon except where this is prohibited in a lease (so a block of modern apartments for example). The property must also be displayed as available on all the websites. Once an offer has been accepted a 7 day notice must be displayed in the local paper, this will read along the lines of;

"the mortgagees are in receipt of an offer of £150,000 for 7 Smith Street, Smith Town, Smithshire. Any person wishing to make an offer must do so in writing to Smith & Co, High Street, Smith Town TEL: 01234 567891 by 5pm Friday the 10th August 2012"

If a significantly higher offer is made by a new bidder then it is likely that it will be accepted as the mortgage lender is obliged to get as much money as possible on behalf of the person they have repossessed. As long as the mortgage lender is happy to accept the delay that changing buyer would cause.

If you go to a house that has been repossessed there should be a notice clearly displayed in the window informing the old occupants who to contact should they wish to remove any belongings that have been left behind. They have 14 days in which to do this. The locks will have also been changed and the letter box will be nailed shut from the inside. So if this house is then nowhere to be seen on the internet and the estate agent says it's already gone there could be something dodgy going on.

The agent I used to work for bought out a small independent estate agents that had two offices so they could expand their company into new territory. Not long after I started a gentleman phoned up asking if we had any "repo's" or cheap properties that he could get at a knocked down price. He informed me that the old owner used to "give him the nod" when something came up. The estate agent would ensure he got it by not putting the other offers forward and would get a nice thank you of about £5000. Easy money if you're willing to risk your business and break the law! This is why estate agents will try and not really let the repossession "hit the market" if they intend on this sort of practice. I must stress that this is now extremely rare but sometimes the temptation of a "back hander" can be too strong for the few rogue agents still out there.

At least now you know the procedures that the estate agent should be following and should be able to tell if something isn't quite right. It is my understanding that the mortgage lenders or the asset management companies dealing with repossessions now conduct mystery shopper calls to check the properties are still being marketed in accordance with their guidelines. It is also prohibited for an estate agent to buy a repossession that is being marketed through the company they work for, or to sell it to a family member or associate.

I think repossessions can be excellent purchases but make sure you're not paying over the top. Don't get involved in a bidding war if you are buying purely to make money. Stick to the target percentages for yield and return on investment you have set yourself.

Buying New build

My views on buying new build may not sit too well with everyone, so before I start I want to state that I live in a modern house. It is warm and energy efficient. It was first bought in June 2002 for £187,500. Four years later it was bought for £210,000 by the people we bought from. We then bought it for £226,500 in October 2011. So the people we bought from made £16,500 in 5 years, not great. However it had original carpets when we bought it, the house was quite dirty (just generally unclean) and the décor wasn't very modern. These house are now changing hands at around £240,000 to £245,000. So you see it hasn't been a great investment for any of the previous owners and not exactly anything to write home about for us. However the house suited our needs and we have made circa £20k in less than a year. I would never have bought this house for investment as they rent for about £950 a month which would mean a yield of 5%.

I would not buy new build, end of.

When I say new build I mean specifically from the builder that built it. The reason for this is because they are, in my opinion, a total rip off. Don't just take my word for it, compare any new build in your area with the equivalent resale property. The resale property will be cheaper, and probably bigger. Better still look for resale properties on the estate you are considering. With very large developments there will often be some properties back on the resale market through an estate agent before the builder has finished selling. I'm sure you will be surprised at the selling prices. Try and always find out the sale price, don't just look at the asking price of the resale comparable.

I appreciate that building companies are there to make money, but they aren't going to make it out of me. If you look closely you will find dozens upon dozens of examples to prove they are a bad investment. In the market we have seen over the last few years people have lost more money on new builds and off plan than any other type of property. It is predominantly because the value is perceived. Builders can put in incentives like 5% deposit, free carpets, upgraded kitchen, free conveyancing etc. There are so many ways for them to try and convince you that you are getting a good deal. Buying a new build can be easy because the builder isn't going to pull out on you and of course, they are always end of chain.

Please remember that this advice concerns buying new build for investment not as your home. I wouldn't buy one even to live in because I hate to think I'm paying over the top for anything (the same reason I will never buy a brand new car, you lose too much money). If you see an individual build and it would be your "forever house" then go for it if its what you want, but never as an investment, just don't do it.

The one and only exception to this rule is buying off plan in a rising market. In this scenario you want to be securing your price 12 to 18 months before the build is finished. If you get in nice and early in a rising market then you could make good money. But again, I would only do this if it was a small individual builder on a select development and I was going to live there.

Buying Below market value (BMV) property

There are many companies online offering BMV property, some just require an email address to sign up to and others require a monthly or one off fee. Some will try and show that they are more exclusive. I am a firm believer in educating yourself as much as possible and hope that this is just one of many books on property you have read, or will read.

Some sites I have signed up to offer BMV of 10%-15% and others will offer 25% to 40%. The website that is offering 40% is unsurprisingly on new build apartments. The 25%-30% were predominantly in the very north of England and Scotland. You also need to be very careful of "certified valuations". The only way to make sure you are getting a genuine discount is to do your own due diligence and use data from land registry on similar properties to establish what they actually sold for.

I attended a seminar once where the company holding it were trying to get us to sign up to their "exclusive BMV deals". This was slightly different to the normal approach whereby the company will try and sell deals directly to the attendees. What they wanted to do was for us to sell the deals to our landlords and we would get a £2000 fee for the introduction. The total purchase fee was £5000 as well as the normal legal costs. So we needed to see if this was genuine before we took this to our database of clients who trusted us. This initial day long meeting was followed up with paperwork and further telephone calls before they finally came to visit the office and give us our log in details to access their website with all their exclusive BMV deals at 25% discount. This company had told us they had connections with banks and builders throughout the country that would offer them massive discounts because they had the facility to bulk sell.

Before the office visit my business partner and I conducted some due diligence on the company using companies house and Googling one of the directors. We discovered that his background was in used car sales and he still traded as such. The company had been formed less than a year and as such no accounts had been filed as yet. We felt it was unlikely such a new company could have built up such vast connections so quickly.

Once we had our log in details for the website the first thing we did was punch the postcodes of the "BMV" properties into rightmove to see what the open market value was like. We found property after property (all quite similar) that were being marketed around or just over the claimed "BMV" price, on rightmove! It would appear they were, to some degree, trying to prey on the investor who was happy to trust and happy not to check. We would have saved a lot of time if we had just been allowed to see some examples of these "deals" straight away.

I would steer clear of these sorts of companies although I am sure there are those that are genuine, you just have to wade through the unscrupulous ones to find them! I do believe there is massive merit in companies that provide investor mentoring or networking because meeting with like minded people and comparing notes can keep you on your toes. I don't have as much time to do this sort of thing as I would like with running a business and a young daughter but I intend on doing more of this type of thing in the future. I subscribe to many newsletters, watch you tube videos and probably read at least one property book a month.

Look at BMV as a numbers game. If you only want one really heavily discounted property a year then I think it is feasible to get up to a 25% discount, in areas where the housing market is struggling more it will become even easier. At the end of the day you could view 100 properties, offer on 30 and get 1 deal. That 1 deal might be enough for you. You will however, need the time to dedicate to this method.

Getting a 10-15k discount and then adding 10-15k in value is a route that I have used and not had to spend so much time.

Stepping in when a sale has fallen through

This is a time when the investment buyer can save the day (and also get a great deal for him/herself). You will read in the next chapter about building rapport with estate agents and how that can lead to them coming to you but there are ways of seeing if a property has fallen through. Sure if you knew a particular property had a "Sold STC" flash on the website and then next day it was back to for sale then you would know it had fallen through. However it would be difficult to monitor hundreds of properties and know just by looking at them.

When I browse rightmove I do it with Firefox as my browser (which is an alternative to internet explorer for those who are, like me, not at all techie). I then recommend you download "Property Bee" which is an application that links to rightmove and gives you all the historical data as you browse. All the info just sits in a box under each property where the agents brief description of the property is. It tells you when the property was first listed (quite useful if it's been on six months), it gives all status changes such as price and also if the status has changed from "For sale" to "Sold STC" and back to "For Sale" again, brilliant!

This means you can keep a simple follow up system for properties that you think meet your criteria and check to see if they fall through. You could then take it a step further and find out once the sale has gone through what was paid. The more information you can gather and the better your knowledge, the better a property investor you will be.

Take a look at the following screen shot and look at the information at hand!

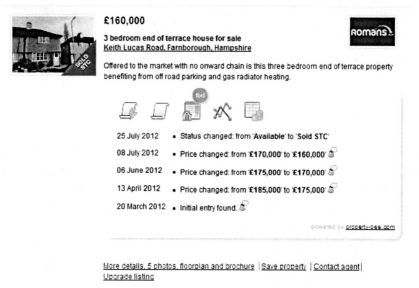

£160,000

3 bedroom end of terrace house for sale
Keith Lucas Road, Farnborough, Hampshire

Offered to the market with no onward chain is this three bedroom end of terrace property benefiting from off road parking and gas radiator heating.

25 July 2012	• Status changed: from 'Available' to 'Sold STC'
08 July 2012	• Price changed: from £170,000 to £160,000
06 June 2012	• Price changed: from £175,000 to £170,000
13 April 2012	• Price changed: from £185,000 to £175,000
20 March 2012	• Initial entry found.

powered by property-bee.com

More details, 5 photos, floorplan and brochure | Save property | Contact agent| Upgrade listing

Marketed by Romans, Farnborough. Telephone: 01252 550800

As you can see this property was initially put on the market on 20th March 2012 at £185,000. The property then came down in price in various increments until the final reduction on 8th July 2012 to £160,000. A 13.5% reduction from the original asking price. It then sold less than 3 weeks later. If you had been tracking this property it would have definitely been time to jump in when it came down to £160,000. You can then use this as a benchmark for other properties in the area. If you use this facility to track property activity you could have a very healthy number of properties in your follow up system to keep an eye on. A very powerful tool.

Summary

- Sort out your deposit and how you are going to get it
- Understand the pitfalls of leasehold property
- Know what sort of property you are targeting
- Keep a follow up system to monitor sales that fall through
- Find your own discount but if you are using a BMV company, make sure they are genuine

3
How to negotiate your purchase

In a way negotiating your purchase starts whilst finding your property. This is because you need to get key information about the properties before (or whilst) you view them. Getting the right property at the right price can be a slow process at times. Some investors will play the numbers game. They will view 50 properties, offer on 20 and maybe get 1. They might have to view a 100 and offer on 40 or 50 to get the one they want at the right price. It all depends on how strict your criteria is, what yield you want and what discount you want. But it is important to have a strategy.

I will share with you my current strategy but please remember that what is right for me may not be right for everyone. This is just what I do and this may well change over time. My current strategy is the following:

- **Get £10,000 to £15,000 discount from what similar properties have recently sold for.**

- **Buy dirty properties or ones that can be easily improved with décor, cleaning and new carpets. Aim to add a value of £10,000 for when the property will be due for remortgage.**

- **Make sure the property will give a minimum gross yield of 7.5%.**

- **Unless a very healthy (long) lease and low maintenance charges (or a phenomenal deal), I try and stick to Freehold.**

You need to decide on what your strategy will be and stick to it. Don't keep chopping and changing or bend your rules by getting emotionally involved with a property. If the numbers don't work with your strategy, don't buy it. It can be very tempting to just raise an offer another few thousands pounds to clinch a deal or compromise and agree a purchase that equates to a 7.1% Gross yield when your rules are you need 7.5%. It can be a slippery slope and will test your self discipline. Devise your strategy before you start and sit down with your business partner (if you have one) and agree on what your rules will be.

Having a strategy in place can be half the battle because as long as you can stick to it then the strategy can dictate your decisions for you. Knowing at what level you will or won't buy will help you relax and approach negotiations with a clear and calm head.

Estate Agents

You need to get these guys (or girls) on side, really you do. Give them a little respect and don't tell them something is overpriced or nitpick on viewings. I can tell you from first hand experience (and you probably have experiences of your own on this subject) that the second I get someone giving it the big "I am" I find it annoying. Even with showing tenants a property let alone with people looking to buy they say things like "the landlord will have to sort that out", or the other classic "that's illegal" with regards to something that's perfectly legal. When someone starts saying to you "the landlord will have to decorate all this, and look at these walls all uneven" (on a Victorian property) you just think "well I'm not letting it to you mate, you'll be a nightmare tenant, hassle for me and hassle for the landlord". Plus you know another tenant will let it just as it is because the property is in fact fine.

So don't tell an agent how to do their job or criticise them in any way. I'm sure they won't tell you how to do your day job, if you have one. It may be that you know more than them about buying a property, a lot of the younger estate agents may not own their own home or have ever bought a property. However if you don't have the agent on side then they won't be underlining the benefits of you as a great buyer to the vendor. These advantages would be having no chain and the fact you will follow through on the purchase.

The approach I use with agents has to be a bit different because I am in the business. I always give my company name and tell them I'm in the business so that they don't think I am trying to steal their instructions, even though we only do lettings. I am then quite specific about the sort of property I want. However, in most cases there is a specific property I have seen on rightmove and want to arrange a viewing. But before I book the viewing first I have to try and establish if it is worth my time making the viewing. This is unless you have the time on your hands to do the volume approach of 100 viewings, 40 offers, 1 deal (maybe).

So, as I said I don't want to come across as the big "I am" so I mention I have a "couple of buy-to-lets" in a similar area and managed to get them at a decent price, yields are good in that area blah blah blah and have a bit of a chat. Whilst doing this you need to find out what the sellers situation is.

Have they found somewhere to move to?

If so is there a chain?

Why are they selling?

If it is "end of chain" or an empty property, are they after a quick sale?

The more you get to know an estate agent and build rapport and trust the more information you will get.

So it may be that on this occasion the seller definitely wants the asking price and has rejected some previous offers. It is unlikely that you will get this level of knowledge without going on a viewing as a viewing gives you a better environment with which to chat with the agent in an open and relaxed fashion. It is not a bad idea to go on lots of viewings and get to know the agents, especially if you are just starting out.

The house I am buying at the moment was the fourth one I viewed and all the previous 3 were almost identical, 2 bedroom ex council houses. What I was able to do whilst chatting on the other viewings was just level with the agents with comments such as:

Is there any movement on the price?

I hope you don't think I'm wasting your time, you're one of the most professional agents I've dealt with but I need to work to a certain price and yield. I know there are deals out there at the level I need them so I hope to be able to buy from you.

If you have any sellers where certainty of sale is more important than price then I could really help. I never pull out of a deal once I have agreed it and I know getting finance is only getting tougher at the moment.

It's a straight 25% down (the amount of deposit), buy-to-let mortgage so the purchase should be quick.

I'm happy to give you my solicitor's details and proof of deposit the same day we agree the deal.

Using comments like the above should start to convince the agent that you are serious, laid back and going to be easy to deal with. No one likes dealing with someone who is full of it.

Just a quick note - An estate agent called me a few days ago to tell me about a property that had just fallen through. As soon as he mentioned the address I said "I thought that was under offer?" He told me that the people buying it ("investors") were a couple and their friend and the friend had backed out on the deal. That would be the last time this agent would deal with these people or give them any decent information or take them seriously. They had just broken one of the most fundamental rules in this business, **don't pull out of a deal.** If I had to give you another rule to stick to it would be - **do what you say you are going to do when you say you are going to do it.**

This agent then went on to tell me the previous buyers were paying £109,000 and he thought he could get it for 104k to 105k for me. Unfortunately I wasn't in the position to buy another property at the time but if I were I would have offered 100k. I told my business partner who spoke to a couple of family members and they were then put in a position of strength with this information I had acquired. All this was achieved through being nice, respectful, not playing the big shot and always doing what I said I was going to do. I was then in a position to pass on this information to people close to me. I believe this all came about because I had done viewings with this agent a few times before although not yet bought through him. I had offered on a property through him a couple of months before and when my offer was rejected instead of telling him the vendors were "stupid" or lecturing him that there "weren't many serious buyers around at the moment" I simply thanked him for his time and professionalism and asked him to let me know if the sellers changed their minds. I said that I would leave my offer on the table for a couple of weeks at the very least and if the property was eventually sold and the deal fell through further down the line then I would still buy the property if I was in a position to do so. None of this can make you look anything other than genuine, patient and easy to deal with.

It was very much this approach that led me to get the deal on the house I am currently buying. I did all of the above and also told the agent the type of property I wanted to buy because you could get a gross yield of 7-8%, which in my area is not that easy on single let dwellings. So the agent came to *me* in the end about a property that had been reduced from 150k to 140k and we did a deal at £127,500. I didn't really want to pay over the stamp duty but I know it is going to value at around 150k after spending no more than £2000 on décor, carpet and some new appliances. It was dirty and smelly and if the owners had bothered to spend a couple of thousand themselves they probably would have got very near the 150k they were asking. Other similar houses were on between 150k to 160k so I managed to get my 10k discount and add 10k value by spending 2k. This also met my rules as the yield is likely to be 8%.

Putting your offer in

When it comes to putting your offer in you will have already established a great deal of information and will probably have only viewed the property if you think there is a deal to be done. When you give your figure to the agent, tell them the offer and then be quiet, don't keep talking. The agent may ask if there is any movement in the offer or try and gauge from you if they can get an increase there and then, before your offer has already gone forward to the seller. All too often people who are inexperienced negotiators will show their hand and say things like, "Try X amount first but we will go up if we need to." I know this sounds crazy but it happens a lot. What do you think the estate agent is going to say to the seller (who is paying their fee)? The agent will say straight away that he can get a higher offer. So give your offer, then be quiet. If you have done everything right up until this point then you will have rapport with the agent and they should just put the offer forward without pressing you. They will hopefully sell the merits of you as a purchaser to the seller as well. All you have to do from here is decide what to do if your offer is not accepted. You can increase if it fits with your strategy or buying "rules", you can wait, or walk away.

Summary

- Be patient, remember some deals will happen weeks or months down the line
- Never back out of a deal
- Stick to your rules and do not bend
- Be polite and professional
- Be clear about what you can offer in return for a property that meets your criteria
- Build rapport, ask questions and don't act like a big shot!
- Build trust with the estate agent and treat them with respect

4
Mortgages and Conveyancing

So once you have agreed a deal you are happy with you need to find a solicitor and apply for a mortgage.

You will have needed to have done some research before starting to view to give you a rough idea of what sort of rates you can get on your buy-to-let mortgage. This way you can run the numbers on any particular property you are thinking about and work out your cash flow.

A good place to start is the internet but if the particular websites you are looking at don't give specifics of the mortgage deal then you may need to go to the actual lenders website as there will be certain criteria. For example some mortgages will be for existing customers only, some will only be for remortgages and some might only be for remortgages for existing customers. Therefore you just need to check that the product you want is for new house purchases. For example at the time of writing I kept seeing a 85% loan to value product (so only 15% deposit needed) with NatWest come up at 5.99% fixed rate for 5 years. The rate was a little high but 85% LTV is unheard of since the property crash. On closer investigation this is for remortgage of an existing NatWest deal only, so just make sure you double check.

Check out these websites as a first port of call or just Google "best buy-to-let mortgages":

www.money.co.uk

www.moneysupermarket.com

www.moneyfacts.co.uk

I also look regularly on the following lenders websites direct:

www.natwest.com/mortgages

www.themortgageworks.co.uk

www.halifax.co.uk/mortgages

So far I have found Halifax and NatWest to be incredibly easy to deal with direct. Applications have been dealt with quickly and I have been getting mortgage offers within 3 weeks. This is essential when following through on the rules of never pulling out of a deal and doing what you say you are going to do (buy the property)!

Buy-to-let mortgages tend to come with hefty arrangement fees at the moment and more so if you are at the 75% LTV end of the market. Both the NatWest mortgage I have done recently came with a £1995 arrangement fee which you can add to the loan. This is quite high but the rates were 3.39% over bank of England base rate (so am currently paying 3.89%) and the same deal which had later been increased to 3.59% over BOE base rate. Despite the high fees these deals far outstripped the higher 2 year fixed rate mortgages on the market. This combined with the discounts I had negotiated made me confident these were the right choices.

My experience of 80% LTV BTL mortgages

My only experience in this field is that I have tried to get one, but never been successful, not on my terms anyway. There are only a few lenders that do 80% LTV. One of which is Clydesdale Bank but they don't take dividends as income, so that was me out. Why not I have absolutely no clue, I don't think they did either. They obviously just don't like self employed people who's companies pay massive amounts of corporation tax and create employment! The other lender I tried was the Leeds Building Society. They asked for a ton of information (which you get used to if you're self employed), which I sent off recorded delivery. This included original accounts, personal bank statements, business bank statements, proof of address and identification. Then, about 4 weeks later and after paying the booking fee to hold the rate they came back and asked for original copies of all tenancy agreements on all my buy-to-lets, bank statement's or mortgage statements proving I had made all the mortgage payments, proof of deposit, 3 years SA302's (I file my account electronically so had to apply to HMRC for these). I think there were a few other bits as well. It seemed to me like they didn't want to give me the money, in reality they were probably just being over cautious. This can be the problem with the smaller lenders, everything has to fit their criteria exactly and anything slightly out of the ordinary can cause problems.

Following the difficulty I experienced with Leeds I decided to get my wife to go into a local NatWest branch and sign up the mortgage on an increased 25% deposit. It was agreed 24 hours later and the survey was booked in. The mortgage offer followed within 3 days of the survey.

Mortgage brokers

I have limited knowledge on applying for mortgages through brokers, even though my wife was a mortgage broker when I met her. She did take care of our first residential mortgage together but these are always more straight forward and I wasn't self employed at the time, also she knew what she was doing!

I don't want to have a rant about brokers or be negative about them but when it comes to buy-to-let there are less products available than for a residential mortgage. Therefore it is easier to research the market yourself online. The only broker I used recently was appalling, they didn't return calls and would return emails in about 48 hours if I was lucky. They didn't charge a fee but quite frankly they weren't good enough to justify charging one.

So the way I see it is this. If you go to a broker, they take all your information and submit it to the lender. If the lender needs additional info they ask the broker to ask you for it. You provide the extra info to the broker and they send it to the lender. The whole way your application is processed just naturally causes delays by having a middleman *and* most brokers charge! I have always found it easier to go direct to the lender, mainly because if you have to fight your corner you can speak directly to an underwriter at the lender. The broker won't argue your point with the lender for you. You might be thinking, what is he talking about, fight your corner? Well, on my current residential mortgage with ING Direct they wanted to know why the figures for my business were so good! They wanted to know why our turnover year 2 was more than double year one and why in year three it had increased a further 30%. I had to explain how the business worked including the residual income from managing properties for clients and the fact that the lettings business (as long as it was run correctly) should always increase year on year. I know this sounds ridiculous but there was no way a broker would have been able to do this as effectively as me. Luckily ING Direct don't offer mortgages through brokers but I firmly believe if I had been going through a broker for this particular application I would not have got the mortgage.

If you are going to use a mortgage broker for your buy-to-let purchases make sure they are an expert in buy-to-let and have their own buy-to-let portfolio. That way you will know they have the necessary experience and can see things from an investor's point of view.

Conveyancing

The conveyancing process is the process by which residential property is bought and sold. It could be useful to have a full understanding of this process and even those of you who have bought property before may not be completely sure about each part. I will chunk down the process into small bullet point stages:

- Deal is agreed via estate agents.

- Buyer and seller provide details of their Solicitor (conveyancer).

- The estate agent issues a memorandum of sale to all parties. (This informs each party of who each other is and which solicitor is acting).

- The seller's solicitor issues a draft contract package to the buyers lawyer, this contains the first copy of the sale contract.

- Meanwhile the buyer applies for the mortgage, a survey is booked and carried out following which a formal mortgage offer is issued to the buyer and the buyers solicitor by the lender.

- Whilst the mortgage process is taking place the buyer's solicitor will look over the draft contract package and raise enquires. These are basically a list of questions, some of which are very standard such as "Is everything in working order (gas heating, appliances etc). Some enquires will be more specific to the particular property.

- The buyer's solicitor will apply for the local searches which should show up anything of concern in the local area such as flooding, or planning applications that might affect the property you are buying.

- Meanwhile the sellers solicitors will reply to the enquires, some of which may have to be referred to the seller to answer as the owner of the property.

- Once the buyer's solicitors have searches, mortgage offer and a contract they are happy with they will send the contract for signing and request deposit monies from the buyer. It is quite common for the buyer to go in and see their solicitor to run through the contract and sign.

- Once all of this has been received the solicitors can phone each other to exchange contracts. This is the point where a legal completion date will be set and the deal is legally binding on all parties. The buyer's solicitor will have had to have contacted the buyer's mortgage lender prior to exchange to order the mortgage funds needed for completion.

- On the day of completion the seller's solicitor confirms receipt of all funds and keys are released to the buyer via the estate agent.

It's as simple as that. But can take months!

Choosing a Solicitor

The solicitor I use for purchases is the same guy I have been dealing with for a number of years. We now know each other and can have frank conversations. If I need to get a purchase done quickly he will pull his finger out. Likewise if I need to buy some time and slow things up he is good at doing that too. This can be handy if I am still saving funds! Recommendation is always a good place to start but I would recommend getting three quotes and also talking to the solicitor that is going to do the conveyancing. You can get cheap conveyancing just Google "Cheap Conveyancing" and there are a number of companies advertising.

I personally have not tried the "budget" route, but if money is tight it could be worth it. You just have to bear in mind these firms will most likely be a call centre type set up and you might not get consistency with always talking to the same person. I like the fact I know the person acting for me and as a result I get a great deal because I not only refer work but use him a lot personally.

I would go with your gut when deciding on your solicitor, but also price should be a factor. I wouldn't pay more than £500+VAT for a freehold purchase. Fees for a conveyance on a Leasehold property are often loaded with an additional leasehold charge of around £250+VAT. I think if you can get a good relationship with a solicitor, in time I would want fees of around £300+VAT or £500+VAT for leasehold. These figures are only a guide on what the solicitors charge is, don't forget all the other disbursements such as:

Stamp duty

This is a government tax on buying property although it is zero up to a purchase of £125,000.
Purchase price of £125,001 to £250,000 = Stamp duty at 1% of purchase price. £250,001 to £500,000 = Stamp duty at 3% of purchase price. Do I need to go any higher? I hope not for an investment purchase! (But its 4% over £500,000)!

Land registry

This is the charge to register the land and title in your name, this information has to be changed on the land registry database by your solicitor and there is a charge to do so, as follows:

Purchase Price	Charge
£0 - £50,000	£40
£50,001 - £100,000	£70
£100,001 - £200,000	£120
£200,001 - £500,000	£270

Searches

The cost of the local searches can vary from around £100 to £250 depending on the area of the country where you are buying.

Bank Transfer fees

Despite the fact most banks now carry out faster payments whereby a bank transfer takes place within 2 hours most solicitors will charge around £20 to £35 for a bank transfer fee. This means the money, that is transferred to the seller's solicitor on completion, is instant and guaranteed.

It is a good idea to add up your total costs of purchasing during your research stage before you start viewing property, this way you will know how much cash you need to get hold of in addition to your deposit.

Summary

- Research mortgage deals yourself first
- Find out if you are eligible (e.g. existing customers only)
- Go direct to the lender
- Know your total costs of purchasing

5
Choosing a letting agent, their costs and preparing your property for let

Whilst carrying out your research for buying you will have spoken to lettings agents so they can advise on rental prices for properties you are considering. As a result you may have come into contact with someone who stood out as particularly helpful or personable. You may have already decided they are the agent you want to use if you have built up rapport and trust. You may have even bought through them if they do sales and lettings. However your research should involve speaking to at least 3 local lettings agents as well as getting a break down of their costs and the different levels of service they offer. You will then be in a position to pick the best agent.

I will give you a run down of the 3 main types of service available for those of you who are looking to use a letting agent. It is a good idea to be realistic about how much time you can allocate to being directly involved in the letting of your property and pick the service that suits your individual circumstances. Regardless of which service you use there will be standard things that your agent should do for you that are a basic necessity of marketing the property.

What your agent will do for you

This should include full marketing of the property on sites like rightmove, findaproperty, Zoopla and prime location. There are lots of property websites but these are the main ones. Your agent should take decent photos and conduct viewings for you. Your letting agent should have already established what you will or won't consider such as pets or tenants in receipt of housing benefit (more on this later).

Once a tenant is found the agent should give you a run down of their circumstances. If the agent doesn't, ask for some background on your prospective tenant. Are they a single professional, are they a couple, a family? You need to agree on a target moving date and at that point the agent will normally take a holding fee from the tenant and proceed to carrying out the references. In the majority of cases the agent will get the tenants to fill out a form (either paper based or online) which will then be processed by an independent referencing company such as Homelet, keysafe or Paragon. There are many companies that do this but the referencing should include a credit check to see if the prospective tenant's have any adverse credit history such as a county court judgment or an individual voluntary agreement (IVA). Either of these could mean the application fails and personally I would steer clear as these types of marks on a persons credit file is basically proof that they have been unable to effectively control their finances in the past. The next thing the referencing company will do is confirm directly with the tenant's employer that whatever the tenant has put on the referencing form about their employment is true, this includes job role and earnings. The applicants start date and if they are a permanent or contract employee will also be confirmed. If the tenant is self employed they should put their accountant's details on the reference form and the referencing company will then confirm directly with the accountant the average of the last 2 years earnings. Referencing companies normally use an affordability calculation to determine if a tenant has the ability to pay the rent which is normally 30 times the monthly rent. So if the rent is £600 per calendar month then the tenant would need to earn £18,000 per year as a gross salary. The total earnings required can be split between two people if it is a joint application. If it is a couple where only one person is working then one of them will have to meet the earning requirements solely.

If the tenant is currently renting then the referencing company will contact their landlord and normally ask questions similar to the following:

1. Has the tenant always paid the rent on time? If not please give more details, are there any arrears currently?

2. Has the tenant conducted the tenancy in a satisfactory manner?

3. Would you recommend the tenant to another landlord?

If the above are answered satisfactorily along with the employers reference and credit check then the reference will be acceptable.

You should be shown a copy of the referencing and if not, ask to see them. You have every right and this is important to make sure what you were originally told about the tenants situation by the agent is correct e.g. What they do for a living and how much they earn.

Once the agent has confirmed by phone, email or letter that the referencing has been successful they should prepare the contract ready for your signature. The letting agent can sign this on your behalf with written authority from you but insist on reading through the contract first. The usual procedure my company follows is for the landlord to sign first (or the agent on their behalf) and then the tenant comes in on the day of the move (or a few days before) to sign the contract and pay the moving moneys. Moving money should always be in cleared funds so cash or bank transfer on the day or a debit card or bankers draft at least 3 working days before.

Inventories

I am going to talk about this now as I will be referring to the check in/check out process and deposits when talking about the different service levels. The one thing I have heard with far too much regularity is "why do I need an inventory when the property is unfurnished?" My answer is, how much would it cost to professionally clean a property that has been left dirty? How much to redecorate walls that have been left grubby or damaged? How much to replace carpets throughout? The answer is, definitely a four figure sum!

In my experience the most common reason for agreeing deductions from a tenants deposit is that the cleaning standard on check out does not match the standard at check in. The inventory documents every detail of the condition and cleanliness of the property including every mark on the carpet or any damage to walls, even dust. So if you have redecorated, re-carpeted and fully cleaned a house, you are going to want it handed back that way or be reimbursed so you can bring the property back to standard, fair wear and tear is allowed. Visit theaiic. co.uk to find an approved inventory clerk and ask them to send you a sample inventory, you will see how detailed even an inventory on an unfurnished property is.

If you come across a tenant who knows their rights then you could be in a position where you can't get any money from their deposit without an inventory. This is because of the deposit protection laws that were introduced in 2007 as the government felt too many landlords were unfairly holding onto tenants deposit monies at the end of tenancies. Legislation was introduced where strict guidelines were put in place that included a route of dispute resolution for disgruntled tenants. I will go into this in more detail later.

Different levels of service

Regardless of the service you use, the process up to the point where a tenant is ready to move in will be the same. The inventory clerk has checked your tenants in, signed over the keys and taken meter readings. The tenancy agreement is signed and all funds taken correctly. So here are the differences on service level.

Tenant find

Typically the letting agent will set up a standing order for all future rent to be paid to you directly from the tenant. It will be up to you to chase the tenant if the rent doesn't come in on time. You will have to liaise with the tenants about transfer of utilities. I recommend putting the service providers in a welcome pack or house guide if you are managing the tenancy yourself so they can put the bills into their name.

Basically the tenant find service means you are now on your own, (although the letting agent may be happy to register the tenants deposit on your behalf) but apart from that everything is now up to you.

The letting agent will normally take all their fees upfront out of the first months rent. You may be charged on a percentage or a fixed fee. Fees will vary depending on where you are in the country and range from a few hundred pounds plus VAT to 8%+VAT of the whole rent for the entire tenancy term. If you opt for tenant find only, personally I would aim for a flat fee and try and get the agent to secure me a 12 month contract. You don't want to have to pay the agent to get a new tenant every six months although this is unlikely as the average tenancy at the time of writing is around 15 months. If you can, try not to pay more than the first months rent including VAT, that way you won't have to send the agent any additional money to cover their bill.

Rent collection

With this service everything is the same as with the tenant find service but the agent will organise for a standing order to be set up in favour of them. They will then charge a monthly fee and forward the remaining rent to you with an accompanying statement. They should chase down any late rent, send out arrears letters and serve a section 21 notice (this is a legal notice sent to bring the tenancy to an end) as and when required. Fees are typically around 8% to 10% of the monthly rent so this does give you an opportunity of spreading your costs and can be a good option for people who are happy to deal with maintenance issues but don't want to have conversations with the tenant about the money side of things. The rent collection service can sometimes come with a set up fee which basically contributes to the agents marketing and administrative costs. Depending on cost you could try and negotiate, my company currently charges £200+VAT for the set up fee.

Fully Managed

This is often the most popular service, especially for those landlords that have a busy day job and don't have the time to dedicate to managing the tenancy themselves. This is basically a one stop shop and the agent will do everything up to and including the rent collection but the job continues once the tenant has moved in.

The agent should transfer the utilities into the name of the new tenant using the meter reading taken by the inventory clerk at check in. The agent will not make sure the bills are paid or set up the payment method for the tenant but they make sure a new account is set up and any relevant welcome pack will be sent out by the gas and electric companies to the tenant. It is then up to the tenant to set up a direct debit and decide on monthly/quarterly/annual payments. The agent should also tell the local council so they can produce an up to date council tax bill, the same applies with informing the water company. The agent won't deal with phone, television or internet services, that is up to the tenant.

After one month (or six weeks at most) the agent should inspect the property and provide you with a written report. This is a visual inspection to get a general feel for cleanliness and make sure the property is being looked after and hasn't been turned into a cannabis farm! This visit is nowhere near as thorough as an inventory or check in inspection and should not be considered as such, but as I said, its more of a general feel. The agent should then schedule an inspection for 3 or 6 months time if all is okay.

With the managed service if the tenant has any issues then they call the agent, even if it is out of hours. The agent should have an out of office emergency procedure, either a call divert or an emergency mobile number on the answer phone. Your agent should be competent in dealing with emergencies. The worst are water leaks or boiler breakdowns (especially in winter). Your letting agent should have a delegated spend limit that will have been taken out of the first months rent along with the other fees. They can then spend up to this amount (normally around £100 to £150) without your authority in an emergency. Personally our agency always checks with our landlords before we spend their money. A lot of agents don't and the first the landlord knows about a deduction or contractors bill is when it is detailed on their monthly statement.

Tenancy renewals

Your agent should diarise to talk to you about offering your tenant a renewal about two and a half months before the end of the fixed term tenancy (whether that is for 6 or 12 months). More about why this is done so early on in the next chapter under "tenants rights". They should also advise on current market rent and if appropriate negotiate an increase for you. We charge the landlord a fee of £75+VAT for a renewal, to cover time and administration involved.

At the end of the tenancy the agent will organise getting the deposit back to the tenant, review the check out report and make sure any tenant chargeable items (such as cleaning and damage) are taken care of and the money recovered from the deposit. This can be invaluable and can require excellent negotiating skills and a calm demeanor.

One of the main advantages of a fully managed service is that the agent acts as barrier between you and the tenant. They have to deliver news to the tenants such as, no they can't decorate the second bedroom bright pink, no they can't get a dog, no you won't replace the carpet because there is a good couple of years wear left in the current one (and other things of this nature).

Important note about the fully managed service

Don't think that just because you have a fully managed service that your agent will take legal action against your tenant for you, you would still need to pay for this unless you have the relevant protection (more about this in the next chapter).

Guarantors

A guarantor will be required if the main applicant (the tenant who will be living at the property) does not meet the criteria of the referencing company. This, in most cases, will be due to income. Therefore any students or single parents relying solely on housing benefit or who only have a part time job will require a guarantor. Normally this is a friend or family member.

The guarantor has to go through the same referencing process as the tenant but the income multiple is normally higher, 36 times the monthly rent instead of 30. They must have a clear credit score or they will fail. Some referencing companies only require a guarantor to be a homeowner but that doesn't actually give them a monthly income so personally I would want a guarantor to be earning. You have to remember that a guarantor will fully indemnify the landlord against any loss (be it rent or damage to the property) that the landlord incurs by accepting the tenant. It is important that the guarantor earns a good income because they will have their own rent or mortgage and bills to consider. If they have to step in and help the tenant it is more than likely going to put an unwelcome financial strain on them.

It is normally possible to have some sort of rent guarantee insurance policy even with a housing benefit tenant, as long as they have a guarantor. I would always consider this type of protection essential if you are taking a housing benefit tenant. It is not that I have anything against people on benefits but it is pure fact that they have to live on a tighter budget *and* have to be able to manage money very well.

Pets

I have had pets in property before and probably wouldn't do it again unless the property was either pre refurbishment, I was getting an additional premium in the rent or the property was properly equipped (laminate or wooden floors throughout the ground floor with a stair gate to stop any dogs going upstairs).

It is all down to the owners really when it comes to pets. If the dog/dogs are well trained then doors and architrave won't get chewed . However when I let one of my properties to someone with dogs the carpets had to be replaced. Even after a professional carpet clean and air fresheners plugged in permanently you could still smell that horrible doggy smell. There was no damage in fairness but it still stank! And what's more, you can't charge the tenant for that because you accepted the dogs in the first place, as long as the carpets have been pro cleaned then you will have to foot the bill. Luckily the carpets were around 7 years old anyway.

I would consider cats but they can scratch and claw carpet. Consider taking a higher deposit and only take pets as a last resort. In the current market people with pets don't seem to understand how much harder they are making it on themselves to rent a property. If you present two potential tenants to a landlord and one has pets, they will go with the other in my experience, without exception.

Using more than one letting agent to market your properties

I have a bit of experience on this subject, from the letting agents point of view. Letting is a totally different area to trying to sell your home as you may find the more competition you have the harder the agent might try to sell your home. However, when it comes to lettings, speed is certainly an element, but it must be combined with quality of tenant.

If two letting agents are competing against each other their first priority will be to let the property before the other agent and the second priority will be to get the best tenant possible. We often compete with one or two other agents to let landlords properties and I'm sorry to say this is the reality. The agent will look after themselves first and the landlord second. This means being first past the post and so the importance of quality of tenant can be diminished. That may be a bit of a sweeping statement but when it comes to getting a good tenant your gut instinct can count for a lot. There are many people that would pass the referencing process but people on low incomes and housing benefit will have to have a guarantor. Not all guarantors will want to (or be able to afford) to pay the rent for the tenant they are guaranteeing. I guess my point is that forging a strong, mutually respectful relationship with a letting agent is the best way to go. If they understand that you only want the sort of tenant that they would want living in their own house, combined with minimum void periods, the relationship will work well. Explain that if they can consistently deliver for you then you will reward them with loyalty, more properties to let as you buy them and that you won't try and knock their fee for every last penny.

I don't think I would ever use more than one agent, even if one day I don't have a letting agency anymore. I would give my chosen agent every opportunity to meet the sort of standards we discussed at the outset and if they slipped for whatever reason I would look for an alternative, I wouldn't use two agents at the same time.

Presenting your property for let

Your buy-to-let property is an investment, so remember to treat it as such. Personally if I was going to do up one of my 2 bedroom ex council houses I would want to do the whole lot on £5000. Kitchen, bathroom, appliances, decoration and carpet. This would not include a new boiler and double glazing. This could cost another 4-5K.

Kitchen and bathrooms need to be of a budget type range, at the end of the day if they are new and well fitted they will look great and be far superior to other older fitments that might be offered by other landlords in the rental market. The same applies for bathrooms. Opt for a white suite, cheap plain tiles can be broken up with a tile border of some sort. Use a shower curtain and rail rather than an expensive screen. Mixer taps and shower attachment are fine as long as the pressure is okay. Often you will need to have an electric shower in a flat unless you fit a pump as there is no gravity from the tank to aid the pressure.

With carpets choose something a couple of notches above the cheapest as these are often so thin they can look terrible. Go for something neutral, maybe with a fleck in it to help hide any spillages that don't come out properly and don't go for cream or beige, go for more of a biscuit colour. Something a touch darker than the usual "new build" finish works well.

With decoration I use standard white ceilings, magnolia walls and white gloss work, it gives a nice clean looking "builders finish".

How much you should expect to pay maintaining your buy-to-let

This will depend largely on whether you have conducted a full refurbishment before letting. If you have, your maintenance costs should be really minimal as everything is new and freshly decorated, in fact they could be zero. If your property is cash flowing well then any maintenance that crops up can be paid for out of the rental income and dealt with by the letting agent if you are using one. Common problems are broken toilet seats, leaks from kitchen sinks or baths, broken or fallen fence panels and broken appliances.

I would allow £500 per year, per property on maintenance as a safe budget. That way if something more substantial comes up on one property (like a new appliance or boiler) then the chances are this won't happen to all your properties at the same time. So if you have 5 properties and £2500 maintenance budget per year then that would easily cover your new boiler. To keep on top of what your actual maintenance bill is each year just keep a simple monthly spreadsheet showing rental income, mortgage and insurance expenses, maintenance charges and profit. You will then know your own numbers.

Something my wife insists on, which has been the cause of a few heated discussions on a number of occasions, is that we have a £10,000 contingency fund that must not be touched. This is a good idea. It is very nice to see the money rolling into your bank account each month from your rental properties without having to do a great deal of work and yes, you do want to achieve a good cash flow. However our cash flow is used as a replacement income since my wife gave up work so it is spent each month. Therefore if we had 2 boilers blow up and property empty for a month our £10,000 could cover all that and we would still have plenty left over. For those who are risk adverse and believe me, I fall into this category, having a contingency is like a child's security blanket. You can sleep soundly at night knowing that even if the worse case scenario occurred (say all your properties were empty for a month and all had major problems at the same time), then you would be okay. Although we both know this is never going to happen ;)

Summary

- Pick the right service
- Be upfront with your agent about what you expect
- Only use one agent
- Make sure you have an independent inventory
- Think twice before taking pets
- Refurbish to a tight budget

6
Some legal stuff

I am not a solicitor and am in no way legally trained (unless you count a D in A-level law). So if in doubt take legal advice but this chapter will give you more knowledge than most (and probably more than most letting agents) when it comes to some of the legalities of lettings. This is all based largely on my own personal experience.

Important stuff about tenancy agreements

The most important thing to remember about an assured shorthold tenancy agreement (AST) is that it is a legally binding document. It should be treated with the respect it deserves by both landlord and tenant. By signing the document and initialing each page you (and your tenant) are agreeing to its contents. Please make sure you are happy to adhere to the obligations within it.

The AST is between the landlord and the tenant. We have heard before that we as the letting agent have "breached the contract", not possible I'm afraid Mr. Tenant, only the landlord or tenant can breach the AST.

Sometimes the landlord will want to put things in the contract that may conflict with legislation. A fairly common example would be for the landlord to request that the letting agent puts within the tenancy agreement that the tenant must give 2 months notice (as the landlord has to) should the tenancy revert to a periodic (rolling) contract. Even if both landlord and tenant initial this part of the contract and sign and agree it, it can't be enforced if the tenant takes advice and challenges it. This is because you cannot "contract out of statute". In other words you cannot put in a contract something that directly goes against legislation. You can put what you like in a contract but if it goes against the letter of the law and the tenant takes legal advice it will be unenforceable. However it is unlikely that many tenants would go back on their agreement to give 2 months notice, especially if they specifically requested a periodic tenancy at the end of the initial fixed term when the landlord really wanted a new fixed term but decided to accommodate a periodic tenancy subject to the proviso of a 2 month notice on the tenants side.

Releasing a tenant early from a fixed term tenancy

With alarming regularity we get tenants ask if they can get out of their contract. Or alternatively they call in and say they need to give notice when they are in a fixed term. So let's clear up a few things about tenancy agreements. We deal with 3 typical lengths of tenancy.

6 month tenancy

This has a start and an end date and this is the usual minimum term for an assured short hold tenancy agreement. If the landlord wants to bring the tenancy to an end at the end date then a section 21 notice has to be served to do that. A tenant doesn't have to do anything other than tell you they are going. If you or your agent hasn't asked a tenant about renewal or got them to sign a new contract then your tenant can, quite literally, give you the keys back on the last day with no warning.

12 Month tenancy

Exactly the same as above but a 12 month term. The same applies when it comes to notice for landlord and tenant.

12 Month tenancy with a six month break clause

If neither party exercises the break clause then the tenancy will just continue for the full 12 months and the same applies when it comes to bringing it to an end (2 months notice for the Landlord and nothing for the tenant). The wording on a break clause can vary but the ones we use allow either party to terminate the contract at anytime after the end of the first 6 month period by giving no less than two calendar months notice and the end date on the notice must coincide with the end of a period of tenancy.

This means if the tenant pays the rent on the 1st of the month they must have served their notice by the last day of the previous month, they then leave in 2 months time.

E.g.   Tenant serves notice 30th September
1st October pays rent.
1st November pays rent.
30th November is the last day of the tenancy.

This is the same for the landlord. So if the other party wants to terminate for the end of the first 6 months then they must give notice at the end of the 4th month. If the tenant decided on the 15th of the month that they wanted to leave (say 6 ½ months into the tenancy) they could give notice at this time but the expiry of the tenancy would be at the end of the month in 2 ½ months time. To terminate at the end of 10 months you give notice no later than the end of month 8, and so on.

Tenants seem to rarely read what they are signing in any sort of depth or give the contract the attention it deserves. In my experience about half read it properly.

So, what should you do if your tenant has signed a 12 month fixed term tenancy and wants out after 8? We have a set procedure in place which has been developed over time which is detailed in Chapter 7. Your letting agent will give you guidance on this which is why I have included the full procedure in the Chapter that deals with landlords managing their own tenancy.

Putting your landlord hat on, not your homeowners head

I hope the views expressed in this book are coming across as balanced, I am not pro landlord and anti tenant, I am pro common sense. This is why it is important to remember the properties you let are investments, they are not the home where you live. This is harder to remember if you let out a property that was a home where you lived. It never ceases to amaze me what landlords think they are entitled to when it comes to damage and wear and tear. I guess that's why deposit protection laws were introduced.

For example, if a tenant put an iron burn on a carpet that is 5 years old, you can't charge them for a new carpet. An iron burn would normally result in a compensatory amount being paid out of the deposit and the inventory clerk should be able to assist on what sort of amount. This is because landlords are not allowed "betterment", the definition being:

1. An improvement over what has been the case: financial betterment.
2. *Law* **An improvement beyond normal upkeep and repair that adds to the value of real property.**

So if a 5 year old carpet has been damaged beyond repair with stains and burns then the landlord is entitled to the replacement value of a 5 year old carpet. Now carpet shops don't sell 5 year old carpet so the calculation would be done based on the fact a good quality carpet would have a life expectancy of 10 years. Therefore you could claim for half the value of a new carpet. Makes sense, doesn't it? And it's fair.

Likewise with décor, the inventory clerk will judge how many little marks on walls would be allowed. If a property had brand new décor before a tenancy and it needed to be redone after a 6 month tenancy then the tenant would be facing a hefty decorating bill, because it had been ruined in only 6 months. However if a house needed decorating again after 5 years, you would not be able to charge the tenant a penny.

The AIIC (the association of independent inventory clerks) guidelines state that a landlord should expect to redecorate a rental property every 3 to 5 years. Are you starting to understand the importance of having your landlord hat on?

You can download a copy of the aiic guidelines at

http://www.theaiic.co.uk/graphics/guidelines.pdf

This whole section about fair wear and tear leads nicely on to another important subject...

Deposit protection

Deposit protection came into force on 6th April 2007. The aim of the new legislation was to make sure tenants who were due part or all their deposit back, got it back. It was a concern that landlords were keeping tenants money when really they weren't entitled to it as the landlords did not fully understand the rules of betterment and what constituted fair wear and tear.

You have to register a tenants deposit in an approved scheme for all AST's created after 6th April 2007 in England and Wales. Any tenancy that was created before this and is a rolling (periodic) tenancy does not require the deposit to be registered. **If the tenancy has been renewed on a new AST then you must register the deposit.**

There are 2 types of deposit protection scheme. An insurance based scheme such as the dispute service (TDS) and Mydeposits and the custodial tenancy deposit scheme called the Deposit Protection Service.

Insurance based schemes

An insurance based tenancy deposit scheme is a membership scheme that allows the landlord to continue to hold any deposit they take from a tenant during the period of the tenancy agreement. The landlord (or agent) will be required to pay a fee to protect any deposits taken from a tenant. Most letting agents who use the TDS will charge the landlord a fee for registering the deposit. The main reason this scheme is used is because the letting agents will have written into their terms of business with both the landlord and the tenant that they keep all interest made on the deposit. At the time of writing interest rates are very low. However the average deposit is probably around £1000 in our area. A letting agent may have 300 or 400 deposits registered at anyone time. That is a lot of interest, if you multiply this across a company that has multi offices (say for example 30 branches), they are then making a lot of money, just out of interest, for doing nothing. My opinion is that doesn't really seem fair, this is why my company uses the DPS.

If there is a dispute over the return of the deposit at the end of the tenancy, the scheme, supported by an insurance policy, will ensure that the amount to which the tenant is entitled is returned. As necessary, the scheme insurers will recover the disputed amount from the landlord.

The scheme is also required to provide deposit dispute assistance which will be provided free of charge to all parties.

www.mydeposits.co.uk

www.tds.gb.com

Custodial tenancy deposit protection scheme

The Deposit Protection Service is the only custodial scheme and it is free to use.

www.depositprotection.com

Therefore any letting agent using the DPS should not be charging for registering deposits. It is easy to register a deposit if you want to register it yourself rather than have the agent do it. Alternatively you can request that the agent uses the DPS rather than the TDS if they are trying to charge you a fee.

Landlords, agents and tenants can all request the repayment of a deposit to the appropriate parties at the end of a tenancy. This can be done jointly or independently, online or by telephone. When one party requests a repayment, the other needs to confirm whether they agree with the proposal, by completing an acceptance form, either online or by post. It is in the best interests of all parties to agree promptly on how the deposit is to be repaid, so that everyone receives the funds due to them quickly and amicably. All deposits are repaid within 5 calendar days of the correctly completed acceptance form being received by The DPS.

An independent Alternative Dispute Resolution (ADR) service, run by the Chartered Institute of Arbitrators, will aim to resolve any disputes quickly and without the need for court action. You have to agree to use the service and it is not quick, but it is fair. If an agreement cannot be reached then each party gets to submit evidence and then an independent and binding decision will be made. The deposit monies will then be distributed in accordance with the judgment. This is why it is so important to have a proper tenancy agreement (AST), inventory and check in/check out process. If you have a fully managed service then your letting agent should take care of submitting the evidence.

What if the deposit is not protected?

If a deposit is not protected, the landlord is breaking the law, unless the tenancy started pre April 2007. The landlord will be unable to regain possession of the property using notice-only grounds for possession under Section 21 of the Housing Act 1988. The tenant can also apply for a court order requiring the deposit to be protected, or for the prescribed information to be given to them. If the court is satisfied that the landlord has failed to comply with these requirements, or is not satisfied that the deposit is being held in accordance with an authorised scheme, the court must either:

1. Order the landlord to repay the deposit within 14 days of the issuing of the court order, or

2. Order the landlord to pay the deposit into the designated account held by the custodial scheme administrator.

The court must also order the landlord to pay to the tenant (or person who paid the deposit on his/her behalf) **an amount equivalent to three times the deposit amount within 14 days of the making of the order.** Ignorance is not an excuse and as you can see, can prove very costly.

Housing benefit tenants

This is often refereed to as:

DSS - Department of social services or
LHA - Local housing allowance

Often a tenant will ask "does the landlord take benefit?" Or sometimes they will refer to themselves as being "on the social". Either way it all means the same thing and is an area of contention.

Some landlords base their whole business model around properties that will attract housing benefit tenants. This is because a lot of landlords see it as "guaranteed rent", after all the money is coming from the local council. However the housing benefit or allowance is paid directly to the tenant, under the presumption/hope that the tenant will act responsibly and pay it over to the agent/landlord in accordance with their tenancy agreement. In my experience most do. There is always the chance they would rather spend it on something else other than their rent though! There is method to basing your business model on housing benefit tenants if, for example, you are buying ex council properties. You may find that working professionals would opt for different areas or types of housing than ex council flats or houses. The ex council houses I own are good value for money (to buy) and offer very generous accommodation and so let well too.

When it comes to housing benefit tenants I would always make sure they can meet the referencing company's criteria and provide a guarantor. I would also go with a gut reaction as to whether to let to them. If you are relying on your letting agent's gut feeling then you need to make sure you have an open and honest relationship with them. In my experience a non working young single parent who is moving straight from a parents house or temporary accommodation into a rental and has never lived on their own would be much riskier than an older single parent, with a part time job who has perhaps just separated from a partner and is used to handling finances and has been out in the big wide world for a while. For me, couples on housing benefit are a no no. I have registered couples looking for rental property before, who have no children and are claiming benefits. It seems the priority is for them to get their own place rather than getting a job. There are enough people in genuine need of assistance through housing benefit without people claiming it through nothing other than laziness.

The majority of people we have dealt with (and let to) who are on housing benefit are young single mothers with one or two children. Using our gut has not failed us yet and the only problem that we get with a couple of our tenants is very slight late payment. This is normally because housing benefit is paid every 2 weeks. This seems bizarre given that all tenancies I have ever dealt with are paid every calendar month. Therefore the tenant gets 26 payments per year and so this can sometimes create a shortfall depending on when the rent is due.

Rent guarantee & Evicting tenants

Rent guarantee is definitely worth having, depending on cost. Some agents will charge up to 3% of the monthly rent to have it. I have a policy on all of my properties if I am putting a new tenant in. This way I can get to know if they are going to be reliable payers and look after the property. I can only comment on the sort of policy I have and how that works but I would recommend looking into this, just for peace of mind. Policies will only normally be available if the tenant has passed the usual referencing process.

So why have rent guarantee?

All tenants can fall on bad times, be made redundant, separate or have some other kind of life changing event that can mean they have difficulty paying the rent. The way the policy works (the ones I have anyway) means that if the rent is unpaid for one month and a second amount of rent becomes due that doesn't get paid, the policy will pay out. It pays up to a maximum of 5 months rent and covers all your legal expenses to get the tenant evicted if they choose not to vacate when served with a notice.

Here is an example of the process:

Tenants rent becomes due on 1st of the month and it is not received.

- A call is put into the tenant to let them know and we politely ask if there is a problem with the standing order.

- If no rent is forthcoming after 48 hours we issue an arrears letter, then after 7 days a second arrears letter and after 14 days a final arrears stating the matter is now out of our hands and the landlord is commencing legal action.

- Paperwork to claim on the rent guarantee is filled out and submitted. The claim is accepted normally after around 7 days.

- Once we get to the 1st of the following month the solicitor acting on behalf of the insurers can issue a section 8 notice. This is a 14 day notice for non payment of rent and after this has expired the solicitor can apply for a court date to proceed to eviction.

- Meanwhile the insurance company will send a full months rent at the end of the second month. This is because the policy I have has one month of excess (this can be recovered from the deposit) and of course, the policy pays in arrears rather than in advance as your tenant is meant to. So even with a policy I would need to find two mortgage payments before I get a payment.

If the tenant comes into the letting agent's office and clears all the arrears then they cannot be evicted under a section 8 notice. The court date (if one has been fixed) will be cancelled and they have every right to stay in the property. Now, bearing in mind the amount of hassle they have caused at this point you may want them to leave anyway, depending on circumstances and how they have conducted themselves to this point. Have they been communicative with the letting agent or stuck their head in the sand? So you may want your letting agent to serve a section 21 notice for the tenant to vacate (this is a 2 month notice) which would mean they still need to vacate on the expiry of the notice regardless of what the rent/arrears situation was. As you now know this notice cannot expire before the end of the fixed term unless there is a break clause in the contract. Just to briefly put things in perspective, out of over 500 tenant moves we have had 1 eviction and claimed on rent guarantee policies about 4 times.

If you have a situation where your case gets to court and the judge grants an eviction notice you need to wait for this to expire and then, if the tenant still hasn't vacated the property, you need to get a bailiffs warrant. The whole process can take an agonisingly long time. The law does seem to be very weighted towards tenant's rights and I can't deny that this situation is stressful even from a letting agent's point of view, let alone the landlords!

We currently charge £120+VAT for rent guarantee which is a warranty offered by my company rather than an actual insurance product, hence us charging VAT. The insurance company then provides the policy to us and charges insurance premium tax. I would challenge any agent trying to charge 3% of the monthly rent and try and get them to throw it in for an extra 1%, or ask for it free for the first year as "that's what other agents have offered" ;)

When serving section notices it is imperative that the correct dates are used and also that when serving a section 21 notice, at least 60 days is given. You have to take into account time for posting and always get proof of sending it from the post office. Don't send a notice to be signed for as tenants can refuse to sign and then it won't be valid. You have to make sure the tenants name is spelt exactly as it on the tenancy agreement. I know a landlord who has multiple properties who only ever uses agents to tenant find who got all the way to court and the judge threw the case out because the date on the notice was wrong.

How much time and money had it cost them to get to this point? I dread to think. Even lettings agents can get this wrong so make sure they know what they're doing and test their knowledge, probe and ask questions. I know for a fact that there are letting agents in our town that just jumped on the lettings bandwagon when the sales market went belly up in 2008 and they have very little experience with this sort of thing. I hope you are starting to realise that good letting agents do earn their money and that you may well know more than some of the less experienced ones once you've finished reading this book!

Tenants rights

There are probably too many to list but one of my main frustrations as a letting agent is the local council. In our area they have a policy of telling tenants their rights. They tell them that the landlord has to take them to court and get an eviction order and that they (the council) can't help them if they (the tenant) make themselves "voluntarily homeless". They tell them all this whilst the poor landlord may be struggling to make additional mortgage payments if they are not receiving the rent payments. To top it all off the council will then phone up letting agents and ask them for properties for people they need to house! It drives me crazy and is just insane. The council are effectively asking us to house a tenant that they will advise to just stay put if they can't afford the rent? Sounds crazy doesn't it? If you have a council tenant, make sure they have a guarantor and you take a rent guarantee policy or warranty (rant about councils over)!

I mentioned earlier your agent should start discussing tenancy renewals around two and half months before the end of the tenancy. This is because if you wish to bring the tenancy to an end at the end of the fixed term a section 21 notice will need to be served to coincide with that end date. My company will serve a section 21 notice if the tenant doesn't come back to us if a renewal has been offered. This notice can always be withdrawn if a renewal is subsequently signed. The reason this is done is because if you just wait for a tenant to come back to you and they decide to leave at the end of the tenancy you may have insufficient time to remarket the property. Also, if the tenant doesn't come back to you and you don't serve notice or chase them down they may tell you they're leaving at the end of the tenancy only a week before the tenancy actually ends! Yes, they can do that. A landlord always has to serve 2 months notice, even to end the tenancy on the end date, a tenant does not.

Summary

- Read and understand the AST
- Know your obligations
- Know your tenants obligations
- Consider Rent guarantee
- Have strict processes in place for renewals and rent arrears
- If using an agent make sure you know their process for rent arrears and renewals

7
Guide for landlords who want to manage their own tenancy

The main issue we find with landlords who want to manage their own tenancy is just that, the management. The most common areas that landlords managing their own tenancy have difficulty with are as follows:

- What can be charged for mid tenancy?
- What is the landlord's responsibility?
- What is the tenant's responsibility?
- What is fair wear and tear? (Mentioned in Chapter 3).
- Dealing with deposit deduction negotiation at the end of the tenancy.
- Being confident enough to insist on enforcement of clauses within the tenancy agreement.
- Property inspections and the resultant conversation if they are unsatisfactory.

The tenancy agreement will outline what are the landlord's and tenant's responsibilities to each other. Some of the key points for the tenant would be:

- Paying the rent on time.
- Treating the property in a tenant like manner.
- Not making unauthorised alterations (e.g. décor, putting shelves up).
- Keeping the garden maintained if applicable.
- Ensuring the property is properly heated and ventilated to minimize condensation and mould growth.

Some key points for landlord would be:

- Making sure the tenant has adequate heating and hot water.
- Making sure all appliances are kept in working order.
- Making sure the property is appropriately maintained.

What can be charged for mid tenancy?

Here are a couple of examples but remember, if you make sure you have a good relationship with the letting agent and you get stuck they might give you some free advice or point you in the right direction. Some agents will just flatly refuse as that is the way they help to bump you up to a managed service. Personally we give advice all the time, as long as we aren't getting constant phone calls from the same landlord who has only paid for a tenant find service we will have a quick chat.

Blocked Drains

This is something that has come up quite a few times. The typical response from a stingy or suspicious landlord would be: "what have they been putting down the toilets? They'll have to pay for it". This is more common if the landlord has a managed tenancy because the agent, not the landlord, has to speak to the tenant. However we cannot just do what a landlord wants and our usual approach on this is to establish a few facts.

First, how long has the tenant been there? If they have just moved in it is unlikely they will have immediately blocked the drains but you must ask if anything like baby wipes or tampons have been put down the toilet. (This is covered in the tenancy agreement and is worded along the lines of *"not to overload, block up or damage any of the drains, pipes etc")*. If these sorts of items are the cause of the blockage you must tell the tenant that they will be liable for cost before the contractor comes out. If I was managing my own tenancy I would make sure the contractor is happy to give written advice of the cause of the blockage.

If the cause cannot be ascertained I would suggest taking a view on this matter. I would pay for the drains to be cleared but if the same thing occurred again during the same tenancy I would inform the tenant that they would be liable. This approach may not take into account that it could be another resident further up the street that is causing the blockage (baby wipes being the most common cause).

Broken Toilet Seats

This is another example. We had a tenant who kept breaking toilet seats. The landlord fixed the first one as you can only really attribute this to wear and tear but then 6 weeks later it was broken again. I personally think its fair to suggest a properly fitted toilet seat should have a life of more than few weeks, say a minimum of 1 to 2 years. Therefore I think this was fair to charge the tenant for the second fix.

When it comes to areas of management there can be a lot of grey areas. The best advice I can give is to approach things with a cool head and try and look at the situation from an outsiders point of view. If you keep cool and calm and the tenant is a reasonable person I'm sure you will resolve any issues. If you really can't come to an agreement you can always split the cost 50/50.

What is the Landlords/Tenants Responsibility?

As I mentioned before this is covered extensively in any Assured Short hold tenancy agreement. Please make sure you read it. So many Landlords and tenants don't read the agreement properly. If you have a decent letting agent this should be very thorough (really a minimum of 18 pages without the additional tenancy deposit scheme terms and conditions). Many estate agents started doing lettings post 2008 when the sales market was really suffering. They often don't fully know what they're doing and some of the tenancy agreements I have seen were about 6 pages long and missed some vital content, really not good enough.

Dealing with deposit deduction negotiation at the end of the tenancy

This is not easy and can take some highly skilled negotiation. In my experience the only reason that this becomes very troublesome is when either the landlord or tenant do not understand their obligations or what constitutes fair wear and tear.

The ideal scenario is for you to get a good inventory clerk and for you as the landlord to present the property properly. If you have had the property professionally cleaned (to a good standard and getting a decent cleaner seems to be a never ending challenge), including the oven, carpets and any gardens having had recent maintenance, are weed free, lawn cut etc then a good inventory clerk will explain that all of this has taken place and that the property must be handed back in that way. Your letting agent can even insert a clause into the contract stating that *"the property must be professionally cleaned to match the standard at check in and receipt provided as proof."* This should make returning the deposit a much easier process.

The last check out I had on one of my properties the tenant had done just this. There were some cleaning oversights picked up by the inventory clerk and so the cleaners returned. Any decent cleaner who cares about their reputation should do this. There were no deductions to the tenants deposit, he knew what was expected of him as it had been reiterated to him on check in and also on email by the inventory clerk when booking in the check out and by us as the agent, he got the message!

So that's how it should be. Something that I have found difficult to express to landlords and also try and give a neutral balanced view on is that everyone is different. Every tenant and landlord has different standards. You would think that a bathroom is either clean or it isn't but some people will pick up on items that others would miss, like lime scale to the underside of taps or a smeared shower screen.

To give you an example we had a very nice young couple rent a property but they were dirty. They just didn't clean. Blinds and windows sills were dusty, they didn't vacuum and it wouldn't surprise me if their bed sheets were rarely washed! One viewpoint might be that if they aren't damaging the property then let them live how they want to live. Another viewpoint would be that this style of living would cause concern when it came to remarketing the property to find a new tenant. I would tend to agree with the second viewpoint. To overcome this issue the agent could have words with the tenant for you if they are managing the property. They could also pull them up on the standard of cleaning whilst conducting the routine property inspections. You have to draw a line in the sand and decide at what point a lack of regular cleaning will start to cause fitments in the kitchen and bathroom to deteriorate, especially in hard water areas.

When a tenant just doesn't realise they aren't looking after a property you could serve them notice if there is a break clause or issue a warning about how they are keeping the property. You could serve notice to bring the tenancy to an end at the end of the fixed term, even if you are only a few months into the tenancy, this would demonstrate that you will not accept the way they are treating the property. You could email them a copy of the inventory, or take it with you if you are conducting an inspection and physically show them how the cleanliness and condition of the property has changed since they moved in and tell them it isn't good enough.

I have also experienced landlords with totally unrealistic expectations of what can be charged for. An example was a landlord that had had his property let out for a number of years whilst overseas although we had only dealt with it for the last 18 months. He came back and in his head remembered how the property was all those years ago. He picked up slight scrapes on the kitchen work surface and minor scuffs to the kitchen cupboards (that you could only see in a certain light) as well as various minor décor points. This landlord must have felt I was entirely on the side of the tenant because I had to disagree with him on so many points. I had to email a copy of the aiic fair wear and tear guide. Sorting out the deposit took hours and hours of my time (luckily it did not go to dispute). What this landlord didn't seem to understand is that the property had the kitchen fitted and all the décor done 10 years ago, 10! Through day to day living a property is going to get marked and very gradually deteriorate. Remember the guidelines are to redecorate every 3 to 5 years (although I would always want to stretch it to 5)! In the end this situation got resolved but I felt the tenant probably agreed to too high a deduction.

On the move in day

If I was managing my own tenancy I would explain to the inventory clerk that I will arrive just before they finish doing the check in. This is the process whereby the inventory clerk runs through the inventory with the tenant and gets them to sign and agree the contents. They will read the meters and get them to sign for the keys. The check in is then attached to the inventory.

Once the inventory clerk has finished I would introduce myself to the tenants and welcome them to the property if I hadn't already met them. You may wish to do the viewings on the property yourself or be present when the agent is doing viewings if you intend on managing the tenancy going forward. This way you will get a "feel" for if you like the potential tenants, gut feeling counts for a lot.

At this quick meeting on move day, make sure you keep it brief, remember they are going to want to crack on and get their things moved in. Make sure they have your contact details for any maintenance issues or problems. Tell them who the utility providers are and tell them it is their responsibility to set up their own account with those providers, including council tax. Tell them that you will give them a call to come and inspect the property in one month. Assure them that you won't be bothering them every five minutes because after the first inspection (that you always do after one month) you will visit every 3 or 6 months (whichever suits you).

A bottle of wine and a welcome note never goes down badly because the tenants will see you are a nice landlord, just be firm when you have to as you don't want them thinking you are a push over.

Property Inspections

A property inspection is not intended to be an hour long meeting with an in depth comparison to the original inventory but more of a spot check of cleanliness and to make sure nothing is untoward. Things to watch out for could include:

- Evidence of people living at the property that aren't on the tenancy agreement.

- Evidence of unauthorised pets.

- Evidence of smoking in the property.

- Making sure the garden is being kept.

Make sure you are firm but fair if you are not happy with anything you find. Follow up your findings with an email saying you will schedule to re-inspect if necessary. Also give the tenant reasonable time to rectify any issues found. Make sure the tenant knows that this is nothing personal and you treat all your tenants the same and expect the same standards. It is only fair if everyone knows where they stand.

So if you are going to manage your own tenancy, bear in mind the above. If you feel you are up to it and have the time (and have found a good tenant) then go for it. You can always approach an agent to manage the property for you if your circumstances change with your available time or if you feel you are having difficulty. Any agent would welcome another property into their managed portfolio especially if the tenant is already in situ. They may even offer you a 0% managed fee for the first one to three months.

Finding good contractors

It's nice to be in a position where you can call a contractor that will go and attend an issue quickly. I had a diverted call from my office recently from a tenant who had no hot water. I phoned a plumber we use regularly, who went out the same night. All this was after 6.30pm. Not only does the tenant think we are highly efficient but it meant I only spent about 4 minutes of my own time sorting out a work issue.

Good contractors are invaluable and they will make your life equally easy and make you look like a highly efficient and considerate landlord in your tenants eyes, if you can find good ones.

What is it they always say about good contractors? Yes you know, the good ones are always too busy. So the first thing I would do is ask for a list of your letting agents contractors once they have let your property, but *before* the tenant has moved in (so you're prepared). Hopefully your agent will be happy to share them with you. You will need a plumber, an electrician and someone for general maintenance/ handyman if you aren't tackling this yourself.

Where we operate (mainly Aldershot and Farnborough in Hampshire) a handyman call out and first hour will be £30-£35. A plumber and electrician call out are £45-£50+Vat. You should be able to find a handyman that is not vat registered as they tend to be sole traders, so this should keep cost down. Its harder to find plumbers and electricians that aren't vat registered but if you can then the bill will be 20% cheaper! Expect to pay at least double these rates in London.

Useful websites for finding contractors.

First off, Google what you want and where but also try:

www.ratedpeople.com

www.checkatrade.com (although please bear in mind at the time of writing I believe I am correct in saying that a negative rating/review will not be posted on the site. This is because each contractor has to pay to use the site and the site doesn't want to upset its paying customers).

Other than this you can try your local newspaper or directory, leaflets from contractors or recommendations. Yell.com is still worth a try to and so is thebestof.co.uk

What if my tenant wants to leave early?

I'm going to cover this here rather than in the legal stuff because the tenancy agreement is between you (the landlord) and the tenant. So if something is mutually agreed, like letting the tenant out of their contract, then that is fine. If you have a letting agent managing your tenancy then they should have their own procedure in place. I will explain how my company deals with this scenario now.

First off, why would a tenant need to leave early? You would be forgiven for thinking the most common reasons are situations like separation of a couple, job loss, job move etc. However in my experience the main reason is stupidity. Yes, really.

We get tenants call in saying "I need to give notice, I'm buying a house." We then have to go and check if they have a break clause or not. If they do have a break clause we have to explain they need to give notice at the correct time (see legal stuff). Or it may be that they signed a new 12 month fixed term tenancy a few months before that didn't include a break clause and so can't give notice. Why do people not read what they sign!?

Essentially these guidelines are based around the fact that (in my opinion) the landlord should not be out of pocket when they are happy to stick with the fixed term contract and it is the tenant who wants to get out of it. Why should the landlord have a potential void period or have to pay an agent to find a new tenant in this scenario?

This is now the procedure we insist upon and we do not bend on any of these points. We once agreed that deductions could be taken out of a deposit and the tenant changed their mind so we were out of pocket. That was silly of us as the deposit is held against damage and rent arrears (not for letting agent's fees)! Once bitten twice shy, so here are our guidelines:

- Any early release from a tenancy is always subject to landlord consent and cannot be guaranteed.

- Early release will be subject to a new tenant being found to replace the outgoing tenant.

- A landlord must not be financially disadvantaged by releasing a tenant early and all associated costs must be paid by the tenant.

  In most cases this will mean the cost of the check out, early release fee and new tenancy set up fee for the landlord if applicable.

- Rent will have to be paid by the outgoing tenant up until the day before the new tenant moves in, even though the outgoing tenant will have to be checked out before that day to allow time for any cleaning and maintenance works.

- All fees will be confirmed in writing to the tenant.

- Procedure will also be confirmed in writing to the landlord.

- If the tenant is in agreement with the above then remarketing of the property will commence once the fees have been paid upfront by the current tenant.

Stick to this procedure and you won't go far wrong. If you are using a letting agent to find your tenant then you could ask them to follow the above procedure and take care of the money side of things.

You may decide to agree a contribution towards letting agents costs if, for example, you had paid the agency based on a 12 month contract and the tenant had only stayed six. You may agree a 50% contribution from the tenant as you have already had the benefit of a tenant in situ for 6 months. I will leave it up to you to decide if you can get away with them paying the full fee!

Problematic tenants

Occasionally you might get a problematic tenant. This can fall into two categories.

1. Someone who is a nuisance and breaking clauses within the tenancy agreement such as not treating the property in a tenant like manner, or not paying the rent!

2. Someone who is just a total pain in the backside and entirely unreasonable.

If someone is breaking the tenancy agreement or is not treating the property in a way you are happy with you will need to approach this is in a calm manner as previously stated. This can be backed up by a final warning if behaviour doesn't improve. If that still doesn't work then you can serve them notice if you have a break clause or be brave and just tell them you are not happy and that you want them to leave as soon as possible.

From my point of view with tenants we have dealt with as an agency we would just not renew the tenancy if they were being particularly difficult. We have a really good relationship with the landlords we deal with and so they are normally sympathetic if the tenant is causing problems and certainly don't have any qualms about them going if they aren't treating the property properly.

Unreasonable tenants are not that common, although the ones that are seem to think because they are renting they get some sort of concierge service, or we have access to plumbers that just sit in our office waiting to leap into action! At the time of writing we have a tenant who is just ever so slightly bonkers. She is proving to be a total pain in the backside saying the property was dirty (which it wasn't as the inventory clerk confirmed on check in), that the property stank, that the loo brush holder was "Just disgusting" and that there were crumbs under the fridge when she pulled it out! Shock horror, crumbs! This culminated in her writing a six page letter to us, sent recorded delivery that we had to sign for, (the flat is just around the corner from the office, told you she was mad) asking for a £50 per month reduction in rent. We will acknowledge the letter within 3 working days as per our complaints procedure and then reply within 15 days. Now, one of two things will happen I guarantee it. 1 - She will calm down once we have replied and just get on with living at the flat. 2 - We will offer to release her from the tenancy subject to the early release procedure.

Tenants can be a pain but it is rare. Don't let it put you off, stay calm and if you really can't take it anymore, let them go. You will always find another tenant and it isn't worth the stress. Do not bow down to their every whim otherwise they will have you popping round to the property every five minutes to do little jobs.

Summary

- Understand fair wear and tear
- You must be confident in dealing with all aspects of managing a tenancy
- Make sure you have the time needed to self manage
- Get good contractors
- Stay calm and be fair
- If it becomes too much you can always upgrade to a managed service or ask the current tenant to leave

8
Guide for landlords who want to find their own tenant

So you have decided you want to go all out and find your own tenant too. The main advantage letting agents have over individual landlords is that the main property portals do not let individuals use their site. They keep them exclusively for the agents so as to not "bite the hand that feeds them". So you have a few options with your advertising.

1. Pay a letting agent to put your property on all the portals they use and just forward the enquiries to you.

Letting agents pay a monthly subscription and it doesn't normally matter whether they are advertising 1 or 100 properties. This is something I would consider but have never had to do, normally because we just "up sell" to a tenant find service explaining we can take care of all the referencing and contract in addition to advertising and conducting viewings. If we were to just advertise on portals only then I would charge an upfront fee for this service and for the administration time taken to forward the enquiries to the landlord. I think this is uncommon because a lot of landlords opt for some of the following alternative options.

2. A classified advert in the local paper.

This is a popular choice for some of the more "old school" landlords who let property for a living full time. Local papers often charge as little as £25-£30 for a lineage advert in the classified section of the paper. Alternatively there may well be a local "free ad" paper where there is literally no cost.

3. Companies that use the main portals but target individual landlords.

This is a cheaper way of getting your property onto the major portals but you really need to know what you are doing to handle the whole process yourself from start to finish. At the time of writing the following sites are offering these prices for lettings:

www.padres.co.uk from £59.95

www.myonlineestateagent.com from £79

You could also consider the hugely popular website www.gumtree. com (which is free), and you are likely to get responses as long the website is actively used in your area.

The next step - Tenant vetting prior to viewings

So the phone has started to ring with potential tenant enquiries. Before you go making an appointment and jumping in your car to go to the viewing you need to get some basic information and need to have established what you will and won't accept such as:

Housing benefit
Pets
Students
Sharers
Children

So the first thing you will do is get a bit of background with questions such as:

1. How soon are you looking to move?

If the tenant has a contract ending in 2 months and you want a tenant in 2 weeks there is no point showing them your property. You may get a response such as "Well I would still like to view anyway". You will have to be firm and explain that you will contact them if you have trouble finding a tenant but at this stage you need someone who can move more quickly.

2. Who will be living at the property? How many adults and how many children?

It is not uncommon for 2 adults with 1 child to want to view a one bedroom property. You may feel this is too much wear and tear and prefer a single professional or couple. In the area I work in (Aldershot) there has been a huge increase in Nepalese people coming to the area (you may remember Joanna Lumley in the press)? Anyway, we have found that they live very differently due to cultural differences and it seems to be an all too regular occurrence that a younger Nepalese couple will move in a set of parents and maybe even an adult sibling. This then means they have people permanently residing at the property that are not on the tenancy agreement and that we nor the landlord were aware would be coming from overseas. As such the property is subject to much higher levels of wear and tear. Not only that, it is best to start a tenancy on the right foot and be open and honest about who will be living in the property.

3. Are you working full time, what do you do for a living?

This may sound quite direct but you will get used to asking this kind of question. It will save you time in the long run. Don't be concerned about a tenant's reaction to this, don't forget they will know that it is likely there will be other people phoning about the property and they will want to make themselves sound like the ideal candidate. In the unlikely event that you do get a response such as "What has that got to do with anything?" It is best to explain that you are keen to learn a bit about the background of any potential tenant and also let them know that they will need to earn at least 30 times the monthly rent as an annual gross salary to pass the referencing on affordability.

4. Are you currently renting? If so what notice do you need to give to your current landlord?

Again this question is linked to timescale but will also give you an insight as to the urgency of the move. If someone is selling a property they would probably tell you if you asked these questions. You could then get an idea as to whether they are looking for a long term rental or just something for 6 months whilst they look for another property to buy.

It is a good time to state your requirements during this conversation, so if you want a minimum of a 12 month contract then you need to say. If the applicant's requirements and your own seem to fit then book an appointment for them to come and view. Make sure you get a name, current address, phone number and email. You can then confirm the appointment time on email and make sure they know where the property is.

At the viewing

It is best to arrive early and if the viewing has not been booked the same day then give the potential tenant a quick call half an hour before you leave to check they are still going to turn up. If you get their answer phone then just explain you wanted to check the viewing was still okay and you are going there as planned. This should reduce the amount of "no shows", which never ceases to amaze me even when following this procedure!

Arrive 5 minutes before the allotted time and if the property is empty then open the curtains and pick up any post. Be prepared to answer any additional questions from the viewer such as how much is the council tax? Would you allow a Sky dish? Where are the local shops, bus routes, train station, road links? It is always best to explain you have had a high level of interest in the property and so it is best for them (the viewers) to let you know as soon as possible if they are interested.

Have a copy of the reference form from whichever company you have chosen to carry out referencing available so you can run through it with the viewer if they wish to go ahead. Here is a quick list of companies you could try.

www.endsleighlet.co.uk
www.credit-check-services.co.uk
www.rentchecks.com
www.tenantref.co.uk
www.fccparagon.com
www.keysafetv.com

You may need to check whether these companies will conduct referencing for non letting agents.

You will also need to decide whether to pay for the referencing yourself or ask the tenant to pay for it. To be honest the references will probably cost under £10 so you may decide to just cover this yourself. Any tenant renting via a letting agent will normally have to pay hundreds of pounds for referencing and administration. We currently charge £420 Inc VAT for up to two people to be referenced. This charge basically goes towards our time and costs. So if a tenant is renting directly from you they will save a decent amount of money, therefore this could be a good opportunity for you to get premium rent. An extra £25 rent per month over a year will still work out less than most letting agent's fees. It might be a good idea to put something like the following within your advert.

"Private landlord, rent direct from me and save hundreds on letting agents fees!"

Once you have agreed a let in principle you should ask for a holding fee, I suggest £500. Explain that this will go towards the move-in costs which will be the first months rent and deposit. You need to give a receipt for this money and it is probably best to carry out this transaction via bank transfer so neither you nor the tenant feel uncomfortable about dealing with cash. You should draw up a simple terms of business to accompany the receipt so that the tenant/s understand that if they change their mind or don't stick to the proposed tenancy start date then they will lose their holding fee. I suggest your terms of business include the following:

- Proposed tenancy start date.

- Property Address.

- Amount of rent and whether it is charged weekly or per calendar month.

- Length of tenancy.

- Any special terms e.g. Landlord to provide washing machine. This should also state that the holding fee of £500 (or whatever amount you decide) is non refundable if the tenant withdraws.

- You may wish to state that if the tenant fails their referencing then you will keep £X amount of the holding fee to compensate for lost marketing time and costs.

It is important that once your new tenant has parted with the holding fee that any further viewings are cancelled and the property is "held" for them. This is how we do things at our letting agency. Once people have parted with money, the property comes off the market. You can explain to any viewers you have had to cancel that you will contact them immediately if anything goes wrong with the referencing for the tenant who has gone for the property.

Once the reference is back as "passed" or "acceptable" you need to make arrangements for signing the AST and taking payment of the first months rent and deposit. I must reiterate again the importance of having a proper AST here. The first flat I ever bought and rented I found the tenant myself, a friend of someone from my parents church. Luckily everything worked out well but looking back I was so naïve, I didn't even get references. What I did do though was pay a local letting agent £100 to do the contract. My letting agency has drawn up AST's for landlords who have found their own tenants and acted as a third party to receive funds and witness the AST. I would recommend you do this unless you already have a tenancy agreement you are happy with and have had it checked (or has come from a reliable source). You will also need to make sure the contract is independently witnessed.

Here are some essential dos and don'ts:

- Sign 2 identical copies of the AST, one for you, one for the tenant.

- Do not hand over keys unless you have <u>cleared</u> funds in your account, <u>ever</u>.

- Do not adjust the AST. The body of the contract should be left alone and any individually agreed terms should be put in an annex at the end. For example, specific terms for the maintenance of the garden.

You must also have prescribed information in the tenancy agreement.

Prescribed information is defined as (and this information is straight from www.legislation.gov.uk)

2.—(1) The following is prescribed information for the purposes of section 213(5) of the Housing Act 2004 ("the Act")

(a) The name, address, telephone number, e-mail address and any fax number of the scheme administrator of the authorised tenancy deposit scheme applying to the deposit;

(b) Any information contained in a leaflet supplied by the scheme administrator to the landlord which explains the operation of the provisions contained in sections 212 to 215 of, and Schedule 10 to, the Act;

(c) The procedures that apply under the scheme by which an amount in respect of a deposit may be paid or repaid to the tenant at the end of the shorthold tenancy ("the tenancy");

(d) The procedures that apply under the scheme where either the landlord or the tenant is not contactable at the end of the tenancy;

(e) The procedures that apply under the scheme where the landlord and the tenant dispute the amount to be paid or repaid to the tenant in respect of the deposit;

(f) The facilities available under the scheme for enabling a dispute relating to the deposit to be resolved without recourse to litigation; and

(g) The following information in connection with the tenancy in respect of which the deposit has been paid

(i) The amount of the deposit paid;

(ii) The address of the property to which the tenancy relates;

(iii) The name, address, telephone number, and any e-mail address or fax number of the landlord;

(iv) The name, address, telephone number, and any e-mail address or fax number of the tenant, including such details that should be used by the landlord or scheme administrator for the purpose of contacting the tenant at the end of the tenancy;

(v) The name, address, telephone number and any e-mail address or fax number of any relevant person;

(vi) The circumstances when all or part of the deposit may be retained by the landlord, by reference to the terms of the tenancy; and

(Vii) Confirmation (in the form of a certificate signed by the landlord) that—

(aa) The information he provides under this sub-paragraph is accurate to the best of his knowledge and belief; and (bb) he has given the tenant the opportunity to sign any document containing the information provided by the landlord under this article by way of confirmation that the information is accurate to the best of his knowledge and belief.

(2) For the purposes of paragraph (1)(d), the reference to a landlord or a tenant who is not contactable includes a landlord or tenant whose whereabouts are known, but who is failing to respond to communications in respect of the deposit.

Pretty boring isn't it? But very important. I'm not sure if you read any of the above but I just want to really hammer home how important a proper AST is. You can buy a pack of 5 pre printed tenancy agreements from the online shop of the national landlords association. They also offer help and advice to members so if you are truly going to "go it alone" I suggest you join.

www.landlords.org.uk

You could also try the residential landlords association where tenancy agreements are free for members (at the time of writing) go to:

www.rla.org.uk

Once you have carried out all the points in this chapter just follow the guidance in the previous chapter for the move in day and about managing your own tenancy.

Here are some useful clauses for the annex. The annex is where you should put any exceptions to the contract. We leave the body of the contract so it will still say about not having pets but then the permission goes in the annex.

Break Clause

The Tenant shall have the right to terminate the tenancy at anytime from the end of the first six month period by giving to the Landlord not less than two calendar months notice in writing to that effect and upon the expiration of such Notice this Agreement and everything herein contained shall cease and be void subject nevertheless to the right of the parties in respect of any antecedent breach of any of the covenants herein contained. The period of two calendar months notice must expire at the end of a period of the tenancy being the (insert date) of the month.

The Landlord shall have the right to terminate the tenancy at anytime from the end of the first six month period by giving to the Tenant not less than two calendar months notice in writing to that effect and upon the expiration of such Notice this Agreement and everything herein contained shall cease and be void subject nevertheless to the right of the parties in respect of any antecedent breach of any of the covenants herein contained. The period of two calendar months notice must expire at the end of a period of the tenancy being the (insert date) of the month.

Decoration Clause

The landlord has agreed that the named tenant(s) can decorate the property provided that it is done in a professional manner and any damage caused is rectified by the tenant at their own expense before the end of the tenancy. Only light neutral colours may be used.

Pet Clause

The Landlord has allowed the named Tenant(s) to keep (insert pet type and description e.g. 1 mature Labrador dog) at the property for the duration of the tenancy. It has been agreed that the Tenant(s) will ensure that the carpets are professionally cleaned at the end of the tenancy and receipts provided as proof. Any damage that the (dog/Cat) should create must be rectified by the Tenant(s) at their own cost prior to the end of the tenancy term. The Landlord reserves the right to withdraw permission for the (dog) to reside at the property should any reports of nuisance be made to the Landlord or the Landlord's Agent by the local authorities.

Cleaning Clause

Even though the inventory and check in/out process will ensure the property is returned in the same condition that it was handed over in, some landlords like to reiterate that a professional clean be insisted upon. You can only really insist on this if you have done it for your tenant prior to their occupancy. The following wording can be used in the annex:

The tenant(s) have agreed to have the property professionally cleaned at the end of the tenancy at their own expense by an agreed professional cleaning company.

Summary

- Decide how you will advertise
- Know the profile of your preferred type of tenant
- Always reference
- Vet tenants prior to viewings to save time
- Cleared funds or no keys

9
Exit Strategy and suggested reading

A lot of people in business feel that you should have an "exit strategy" in mind when you set out on your journey. I can't say whether I would ever sell my business. I think that would be foolish as long as it can create a wage for me and, in time, a passive income whereby I don't work in the office day to day. This combined with the property income should create a very comfortable lifestyle.

My "exit strategy" with property investment is to not exit. I want to pass my property portfolio on for generations to come and hope that my descendants will educate themselves sufficiently to be able to handle the portfolio and add to it, if they chose that path. A basic financial education is desperately needed in this country and my mindset has been changed forever just by reading and continually trying to educate myself. This is why I have included a suggested reading list.

Property goes up in value over time, end of. So why sell? Well, some people reading this might be wondering what happens when they reach the age where the mortgage company will want their money back. Or you may want to have a strategy in place so that you are left with a number of mortgage free properties by the time you reach retirement age.

I appreciate that everyone will have different end goals and everyone will start their property investment journey at different times in their life and have different attitudes to risk and debt. The later you start, the more important having a clear exit strategy may become. So here are some examples to help give you some inspiration for how you may wish to "exit".

Example 1

Geoff starts investing at the age of 40 and buys 10 properties by the time he is 50. He decides he wants to leave a property to each of his 2 children and so seeks professional advice from an expert to investigate gifting or selling the properties to his children.

He then plans to sell 3 of the remaining 8 properties and use the proceeds to clear the mortgages on the 5 properties that are left over. He aims to do this by the time he reaches an age where the mortgage lenders will want their money back. He staggers selling the 3 properties so he can make best use of his capital gains annual allowance. He also plans to start selling off the properties once he has retired as his overall income will reduce and therefore reduce his overall tax liability. This plan will leave him with 5 mortgage free properties providing a healthy income for Geoff's retirement.

At the time of writing hmrc.gov.uk states the following:

Inheritance Tax when passing on property

For Inheritance Tax purposes, giving your home away is treated as making a gift. The rules about passing on property are complicated, so it's a good idea to seek legal advice.

There are two things about gifts to be aware of when passing on property:

- ***Seven-year rule.*** *You can make an outright gift of your home to someone, no matter what it's worth, and it will be exempt from Inheritance Tax if you live for seven years after making the gift. This is known as a Potentially Exempt Transfer.*

- *Gifts that you continue to benefit from. If you give your home to your children with conditions attached to it, or if you continue to benefit from the home yourself, this is known as a 'gift with reservation of benefit' and the gift won't be exempt from Inheritance Tax, even if you live for seven years afterwards.*

The next three examples show three different approaches to investing £200,000.

Example 2

Michelle has £200,000 to invest.
She buys two 1 bedroom flats at £100k each and rents them each for £600 a month.
Her annual income is £14,400 before maintenance and management costs. Her gross yield and return on investment are the same as there are no mortgages – 7.2%.

Example 3

Roger has £200,000 to invest.
He buys four 1 bedroom flats at £100k each and rents them each for £600 a month. He has a £50k mortgage on each property at a 4% interest rate.

Rent income = £28,800
Interest only mortgage cost total = £8000
Annual income = £20,800 (before maintenance and management costs).
His yield is still 7.2%
His ROI is 10.4% (£20,800 divided by his £200,000 investment)

Roger uses enough of his rental income to clear down the mortgage on one of his properties in time for his retirement. He then sells one, which because of capital growth, has enabled him to clear the mortgage on the 2 remaining properties with the sale proceeds. He is now left with 3 debt free properties.

Example 4

Louise has £200,000 to invest.
She buys 8 one bedroom flats for £100k each with a £25K deposit on each at an interest rate of 4.5%. The rent is £600 a month on each.
Rent income =£57,600
Interest only mortgage cost total=£27,000
Annual income=£30,600 (before maintenance and management costs).
Her yield is still 7.2%
Her ROI is 15.3%

Louise has bought her 8 flats by the time she is 45. After all costs and tax her annual income is £20,000. She uses this money to pay £2500 off each £75k mortgage per year. This reduces her interest payments by £900 for year 2 which she puts aside in a separate account for refurbishment. Each year the money saved in interest payments by reducing the mortgage is put aside and she continues to pay off £2500 off each mortgage. Over 20 years she pays off £400,000 worth of mortgage debt leaving her with only £200,000 to clear. All the properties have doubled in value to £200,000 so she sells one and clears all remaining mortgage debt. Her rental income for the year easily covers her capital gains liability on the one sale and she is left with 7 mortgage free properties worth £1.2 Million and a very, very nice retirement.

The following chart may help represent the first 5 years of this example more clearly:

	Total Rental Income	Total Mortgage amount	Profit after costs including mortgage payment	Interest only payment	Amount paid off mortgage debt at year end	Money put in "refurb" pot
Year 1	£57,600	£600,000	£20,000	£27,000	£20,000	£0
Year 2	£57,600	£580,000	£20,900	£26,100	£20,000	£900
Year 3	£57,600	£560,000	£21,800	£25,200	£20,000	£1800
Year 4	£57,600	£540,000	£22,700	£24,300	£20,000	£2700
Year 5	£57,600	£520,000	£23,600	£23,400	£20,000	£3600
Total	£288,000	£500,000	£109,000	£126,000	£100,000	£9000

I appreciate that each year your costs and rental income are not going to stay exactly the same but hope you will understand this is not the purpose of this illustration. This chart doesn't take into account rent increases which one could argue may cover any void periods. In this example Louise has £9000 extra cash after 5 years due to the increase in profit from reducing her mortgage debt. She spends £5000 of this on redecoration of the apartments and replaces a kitchen in one apartment and 2 bathrooms with the remaining £4000.

I wish you the very best of luck with your property investment future. There are enough good deals to go around at the moment but I firmly believe that NOW is the time for action. Leave it another couple of years and we may well be out of this recession and you could be competing with first time buyers and uneducated first time landlords that don't know what you know. That could be the time when people who take action now could be sitting back and watching their equity increase nicely year on year, or even month on month like it did in 2007. But a lot of investors like me and people that get involved now will seriously slow up the pace of buying as house prices improve. As the market accelerates on and everyone else starts buying you must be cautious.

Remember, observe the masses and do the opposite!

"Be someone that makes things happen, even when others tell you it can't be done" – Richard J Oldaker

If you feel it would help, I can work with you.

If you have liked what you have read and the principles outlined but would like the security of me walking through the process with you then myself and my business partner do carry out a property finding service. Please get in touch via my company website and I will contact you to discuss availability and the services we offer.

A more hands off approach?

My business partner and I are in a position where (at the time of writing) we see many deals that fit our criteria and are not in a position to buy them all. We are happy to work with you and find a property based on your specific criteria. The property will meet a minimal yield, come with instant equity and we can let the property out for you and manage it if required through our agency. I would not recommend managing a tenancy yourself unless you are local to the property. If you are happy for us to manage the tenancy then we can find you a deal in Aldershot or Farnborough and take care of the whole thing.

If you would be interested in this truly simple and profitable way to get into property investment, or extend your current portfolio just contact us via our website www.richardjamesinvestments.com

Suggested reading

Rich Dad Poor Dad by Robert T Kiyosaki
This is essential reading as far as I am concerned and is also good for mindset and reassuring you that what you are doing is the right thing (even if it is not what nearly everyone else does)!

The Richest Man in Babylon by George S Clason
This has stood the test of time and is a very quick read, another essential.

How to make cash in a property market crash by Rob Moore and Mark Homer
This is a great read, definitely one of the better property books out there.

Think & Grow Rich by Napoleon Hill
Another classic referred to again and again by modern authors.

Awaken the giant within by Anthony Robbins
A monster of a book but great for taking control of all areas of your life, getting you happy and generally giving you a kick up the backside.

List of websites

www.google.co.uk

www.rightmove.co.uk

www.zoopla.co.uk

www.property-bee.com

www.money.co.uk

www.moneysupermarket.com

www.moneyfacts.co.uk

www.natwest.com/mortgages

www.themortgageworks.co.uk

www.halifax.co.uk/mortgages

www.theaiic.co.uk/graphics/guidelines.pdf

www.mydeposits.co.uk

www.tds.gb.com

www.depositprotection.com

www.ratedpeople.com

www.checkatrade.com

www.yell.com

www.thebestof.co.uk

www.padres.co.uk

www.myonlineestateagent.com

www.gumtree.com

www.endsleighlet.co.uk

www.credit-check-services.co.uk

www.rentchecks.com

www.tenantref.co.uk

www.fccparagon.com

www.keysafetv.com

www.landlords.org.uk

www.rla.org.uk

www.legislation.gov.uk

www.hmrc.gov.uk

Acknowledgements

It's nice to be able to put down in black and white a few thank you's so here goes. Firstly my wife Emma, for always supporting me, loving me and putting up with me, even when I have spent what little time we seem to have together at the moment writing a book! Thanks to Ella for always having a smile for me in the morning and being the best little baby ever! Thanks to my mum and dad for their unconditional love and support. They supported me when I decided to go to work instead of university and, despite reservations, supported the decision to buy my first property at 19 years of age. Thanks to the rest of my friends, family and especially to those individuals who proof read this book. Thanks to my business partner James for having the balls to open a business with me (even though he was only 23 at the time). Thank you to any landlords past and present who have used my/our services. James and I really do our best to deliver a great service and last but certainly not least, thank you for buying and reading this book.

Notes